Mario Persona

Moving On

Other books by Mario Persona (Portuguese):

Crônicas de uma Internet de Verão (2001)
Receitas de Grandes Negócios (2002)
Gestão de Mudanças em Tempos de Oportunidades (2003)
Markeging Tutti-Frutti (2004)
Marketing de Gente (2005)
Dia de Mudança (2007)

Mario Persona

Moving On

Out-of-the-box wisdom for your career in this ever changing world

1st. Edition — 2007
©2007 by Mario Persona
contato@mariopersona.com.br
www.mariopersona.com.br

Credits:

Translation: Marcos Zamikhowsky Lopes
Proofreading: Marilyn Gorgas-Cahill
Cover Design: Stephan Dirck Klaes
Cover Photograph: Clayton Hansen — istockphoto.com/claylib

Contents

Letter to an executive

Hi, Joe. No need to say Mr. Smith; I'll just call you Joe, because that's all you once used to be. I want to talk to you. Can I have five minutes of your time? Two? I know that you don't have time, that you're in a mad hurry, but what I want to say is important just so you don't continue to be this way — mad — when the rush is over.

It's true, the rush will be over; nothing lasts forever. How many times recently have you heard the phrase *"He doesn't work here anymore"* when you called someone? It didn't use to be like that, did it? These are new times. Be humble. Much of what you think you have isn't yours. It belongs to the company or to the position you have.

Remember Junior, the guy full of MBAs, who could even speak Mandarin? Look, Joe, you'd better lose some weight, because he's going to take over your jacket. You used to be the cream of the crop, but not anymore. Things have changed. A hundred days without results and somebody else is going to be picking up the phone at your office and saying: *"He doesn't work here anymore."*

You'll get the red carpet exit, all right. After all, the company has an image to preserve. They'll say you left in order to develop your own projects (which means *"look for a job"*), to seek new challenges (*"look through the job ads"*) and to have more time for the family (*"be supported by the wife"*).

So start getting off your high horse, because, for one thing, it's not your horse, it's a rental. Maybe it's not your job on the line; maybe it's your employer's. Businessmen also get fired. By the market.

When I was young and was working for a bank, I negotiated the renewal of the bank's lease with the property owner. There was a lot of money involved.

Smoking a cigar and bored with the deal over the huge table in a huge office of the huge building of his huge company, he puffed in my face the very high-and-mighty conclusion:

"Suit yourself, let's keep it at that. This rent is what I spend on fuel for my yacht on a weekend."

His yacht must have been really big and burned up quite a bit of fuel, because a few years later he had no yacht, no company and no cigar. Only smoke. Times have changed, so be humble, Joe. What do you mean, be humble?

Well, steer clear of the image of an executive I once saw playing golf at a resort. Lofty and arrogant, blaming others for his golfing mishaps, he was quite a show. He drew attention to himself with his temper tantrums, cursing the grass and blaming it for his failure to get the ball in the hole. That was a few years ago. I don't know how he's been doing since.

You probably won't retire as an executive. Few people will make it to that point. Get used to the idea of not being at the next convention to see Peter Drucker and other gurus. For one thing, even the great Drucker is gone, like everyone else will be one day, and so will you. So be humble.

Learn to live like a simple mortal — stay in line at the bank, take the bus. It may not have the glamour that you're used to, but it's less stressful than the life you're leading now. By the way, remember to leave the glamour at the reception desk along with the badge. It belongs to the company.

Don't get carried away by your network of friends. Many of them go with the flow. When you're no longer a hot investment, they just won't be around. Then it might be the right time to call all those business cards you kept for a rainy day. But don't be surprised if what you hear mostly is: "He doesn't work here anymore."

Start developing a "Plan B," a "Plan C," or maybe even a "Plan Z." The more options the better. You might end up a consultant or even a professional speaker like me. You can't imagine what kind of CVs some people who look for me have. They're after tips on how to give lectures, figuring this is the standard retirement of every executive. It's hard to believe that I may have something to teach people with that kind of background.

Identify your capabilities. Is there anything you know how to do? I don't know, cooking, sewing, or book-keeping? These skills can be pretty useful when you start your own business as a restaurant owner or swim-suit manufacturer, or stay home doing the accounting for your new clients. OK, you can present yourself as a *"chef," "fashion designer,"* or *"personal finance coach,"* when you do the tax return for friends in your *"home office."* You can use these terms if you want to add some glamour to your new activities. But if you don't know how to do anything, be humble and go back to studying.

I have no more tips. Oh, yes! One more: be humble. I've said that? All right, it's my age. And, by the way, what is yours? You know it matters, don't you? Speaking of humbleness, I know businessmen and executives who've worked that way, providing an example of hu-mility and making the act of serving into a trademark of their professional image.

During lunch at an event, the owner of an industrial group that had hired me interrupted what he was doing to greet me. What he was doing? Serving tables. An-other one, a CEO of a multinational company, took my suitcase and carried it to my car in the hotel parking, before the flabbergasted eyes of those who follow his daily orders in the company. Aloof managers will dis-appear. Those who don't mind rolling up their sleeves and doing a little manual labor will survive. So be hum-ble.

I know, I've said it already.

Introduction

I visited her in Philadelphia, even though I knew she was in a terminal condition. The experience wasn't very pleasant; it brought only memories of better days. I reckoned I wouldn't have another chance if I didn't see her on that one cold North American early-winter morning.

I felt a mix of reverence and sadness as I passed through those heavy doors. It was like invading a pharaoh's tomb, centuries beyond its glory days. Like ancient hieroglyphics, the lettering on the walls screamed the agonizing message: "GOING OUT OF BUSINESS!". I was actually in one of the Towers Records chain shops, another casualty of new times and changes.

Have you realized how quickly things are changing? As a youngster, going to a record store was a major event. It was also a pain because some shop owners had the sadistic habit of pretending they didn't understand the name of the song and asked us to sing a part of it. I really hated that, but I liked to drop by, just to hear another jerk sing. It was hilarious.

That's in the past. If there's still a music store in your town, rush over and take the kids. Someday they'll be able to say they've been to such a place, in much the same way I can tell today I've ridden in a cable car.

CD Stores are biting the dust, but not all by themselves. Photo shops are going down with them. Everything's digital now. You take pictures with your cell phone and have them printed via the Internet. Music? Just download it. And what about the video from the rental store? It's kicked the bucket and is awaiting the band to play at the funeral. The Broad Band.

Oddly enough, the one that seemed to be at death's door holds on strong and firm. Older — much older — brother of other media of artistic expression, the book is still outsmarting death and scoring goals.

When the first personal computer came up, everyone thought that it would be the final nail in the book's coffin. No one thought about sound or image, since the first machines could only sing *"beep"* and print photos made of letters. But traditional image and sound media passed away first. Meanwhile, all attempts to separate letters from paper media failed to get the seal of approval from the ultimate judge, the market.

The book is a fetish. People want to feel its cover, leaving marks as they slide their fingers through its pages, show it off on the way to work or on a bookshelf. Some bookstores even sell books by the foot, just for ornamental appeal. I saw a guy in a bookstore, looking at himself in the mirror as he catwalked, modeling a book. He chose the one with the best-looking cover, probably just to take it for a walk.

So far, so good. The trouble is dealing with the amount of people who write to me wanting to know how to publish a book. They think you're only a writer if you get your book in print. Not true. A writer is someone who writes, just like a sculptor carves, a painter paints and a singer sings. One shouldn't be concerned about whether the world will get to see one's work. To a writer, putting words in paper is a physiological need, a visceral one. Writing is the emesis of the satiated bee; it's the honey.

The mistake lies in thinking that getting your book printed is synonymous with becoming rich and famous. People in this mind frame don't really want to become writers; they want to become rich and famous. Most published writers don't even come close. For one thing, you have to enjoy reading. If you hate reading, forget it. Or hire a ghost-writer. You like writing? Start doing it. That's how I got started.

But, since everything is changing ever so rapidly, I write in a way I could never have done in the past. This book is a *blook*. Blook? That's right; the word comes from *blog+book*, a book printed with an assortment of texts published at first in a blog. Lots of people are now writing this way. In these pages, I gather a selection of texts that I published on the Web as the ideas sprouted. After that, all I had to do was select, compile, improve this, expand that, update and... *Presto!* Here's the blook.

I don't think the old-fashioned style of writing — starting at the beginning, going through the middle and getting to the epilogue — will ever end. The thing is, good ideas aren't always all in the mind of the writer, and the blog is a kind of daily mental corkscrew that helps keep a book alive, even if the author has no intent of writing it as a book. Call it a notepad or a virtual rough copy if you like. Sound weird to you?

Well, just wait till you read what's next. This book is being initially published on demand. After releasing six books in Portuguese by a traditional Brazilian publisher, I decided to try what I view as the next great trend of the publishing sector. Books are being produced and sold like bouquets from online flower shops. You access a flower site located in, say, Los Angeles, and send a bouquet to someone in Shanghai. A half-hour later, the recipient receives the flowers that were, in fact, packed and delivered by a Shanghai flower outlet linked to the site in Los Angeles.

There is no stock of books, only digital files that are turned into books at the place and time of purchase. This will have enormous impact on publishing houses, as literary output follows in the steps of musical production. Any band that is presently unable to break into the market through traditional means can make their music available for download and, depending on its success, might even be found by an agent and later hired by a renowned record label. Likewise, any author can now put their books up for sale in a matter of hours and, who knows, may be discovered in the traditional editorial circuit.

Not only has the book changed, so have films and records. The world around us is changing so overwhelmingly, and that's what I try to convey in these chapters woven with short stories. Why short stories? Well, since I don't know your age, educational background or profession, writing in a storytelling style, rich in metaphors, analogies and parables, allows me to practice role allocation. Your part is to choose the one that best suits you, paying close attention to what's between the lines, which is where I use the most ink.

I could list a million other reasons for my style, but I guess the main reason is that this is the way I like to write, much like someone who chats and tells stories. It's more natural, personal and memorable than a book packed with texts full of academic language, topic lists, charts and graphs. Sure, if you want to impress your boss, who might see the book on your table or the nosy jerk reading over your shoulder on the bus, you'd better find something a little more highbrow. And what are you going to do with my book? Use it for bathroom reading. It's inspiring.

Mario Persona

Moving on

The very day he was moving, from his home and city, when any help would have been welcome, guess who came to give Brent a hand? A relative. Not the mother-in-law, another one. That's right, the brother-in-law. But how was it that he wanted to help just now when the truck was jam-packed? Brent was suspicious. In fact, he was always wary of his brother-in-law, ever since he met Tanya.

When asked why he didn't like her family, he said he just didn't. He had no motive. Brent suffered from a kind of *"Cain Syndrome,"* a desperate need to stay away from anything to do with relatives, causing one to forget that opportunities might come by, even through in-laws.

Months before, Brent had been hit by unemployment. More and more people were getting the axe, and the better the job, the higher the fall. Heads of all ranks were rolling, especially middle management, which was be-ing squeezed out by the flattening of the command pyramid. Blue-collar workers with managerial skills now got their orders directly from the president, and com-manded their own peers, with no extra pay.

Brent knew there was no point in feeling sorry for him-self or in continuing to talk about what he had been in the past. When he realized that, in the big city, jobs didn't grow on trees, he decided to take what was left of his savings and hit the road. After weighing the pros and cons, he decided to move to the country. He knew where he wanted to go, but not what to do. Set up his own business? Render services? Go back to being an employee? He would think about it later. Now, he was only thinking about moving.

The chosen destination was a city in Arizona. It looked like a promising spot, an El Dorado, but for those al-ready there, it was too hot, dry, and dusty.

Tanya, however, suspected ulterior motives behind the move to such a distant location from the coast. His brother-in-law had even offered him partnership in his small pool factory, quite a break for his sister's unem-ployed husband. Brent said he would think it over, but he didn't even call back. Doing business with relatives was not something he believed in. In fact, he didn't be-lieve in relatives. To him they were all snakes in the grass.

Being caustic, Brent's favorite subject (over Sunday lunches at his mother-in-law's place) was the failure of family businesses. He liked to needle his bother-in-law, even though he knew successful ones existed. He had even worked for one, but never mentioned it. It was a century-old enterprise, in its fifth generation. Even so, he kept on bashing them, just to be at loggerheads with them. Not much humbleness there.

It was not long before his brother-in-law let on how he would help in their move to the midland: he would give them a pool, so the children could cool off on hot days. Brent couldn't believe it. It must have been an over-stocked item, or had a leak, he thought. But before he knew it, the pool was on board, upside down and tied up over the load as they jolted on toward Arizona.

Days later, Brent stood dusty and sweaty in the summer heat at the gate of his stuffy rented house. He was the image of desolation: no job, no work, and no swimming pool to swim in. For the pool remained where it had been left on the night they arrived, propped against the only tree shading the flowerless clay garden.

In the city, while everyone else was striking it rich, Brent was waiting. If a break came up, he couldn't miss it. Somewhat distracted, he almost didn't notice the dusty SUV that pulled up to his gate.

"You have a bigger one of those?" asked the rich farmer from the car window, pointing to the pool by the tree.

Brent looked at the pool, at the farmer and, weighing the pros of profits against the cons of family hostility, he decided to take the chance. Sounding like a business-man, he responded point-blank:

"*We* don't have it ready for delivery, but *we* can have it here next week, straight from *our plant*."

Then, after a shower, Brent gave his brother-in-law a call.

Hobby

Today I found out that 29 CDs can be put into a package of *Catupiry*, the most famous cream cheese in Brazil. So what? Well, those backup CDs, presently scattered in drawers, will now all be kept together in that nice round-shaped box At least 29 of them. In the old days, the package for this cheese, created in 1911 by Italian immigrant Mario Silvestrini, was a wooden one, and I used to keep nails and screws in it.

Times have changed, my needs are different, and cream cheese is nowadays manufactured in a way that would have looked like science fiction a hundred years ago. But the Brazilian manufacturer preserved two important things: the flavor and the characteristic Art-Deco label. What could be improved was improved, and what should be preserved was preserved. Now the package is made of white polypropylene, and I have no more screws to put away, because I've also changed. Today I have CDs.

Before you ask, yes, in order to store 29 CDs you first have to eat all the cheese in the package. No, the squeeze-type package is not appropriate for storing CDs. Yes, there is a solution for those who have lots of CDs: try purchasing the 8 pounds bucket. Your fourth question might be: What does all this have to do with my life, career, or business? Everything.

I mentioned *Catupiry*, without having been paid a cent of merchandising for it, to show two things. The first one is that, even if you and your career are constantly changing, the essence of what you are must be preserved. Your label — the reputation people have come to recognize — should also stay on. Sure, this is true only for those who are well-seasoned and have a good market reputation. If that's not your case, then you'd better do your homework before we go on with our conversation.

The shape of the *Catupiry* package remains the same, an analogy I'll have difficulty in applying to anyone my age. My shape keeps changing, for the worse. But let's leave the form aside and focus on the utility of the package. Times have changed, the package has adapted itself, and I've found new uses for it.

Now this applies to you and me. There is always another use for any professional. Some keep on trying to find a position in the same activity they've been in for the last century, without noticing that the market has changed. Maybe the time has come for you to change, to find a new use for the old you.

But is there an alternative use for you? Well, it's always possible to find some profit-making activity with your own repertoire of skills. You have to start looking. The first thing one thinks about in a time of change, of switching to a new job or setting up a business is one's hobby. Is it possible to turn a hobby into a business? Maybe. Some of the most captivating businesses stemmed from hobbies.

You probably know many software professionals who turned their hobby into a job. It makes sense. Most of the people behind the revolution and evolution of computers and systems were young people, and young people easily fall in love with new ideas, like to take risks, and they have more free time available for their ideas. That's the prescription: passion, risk, and time. It's hard to find any kind of positive change that doesn't include one of those items.

A fourth factor, which you might want to consider, especially if you're over 40, is meaning. Until the age of forty, we're too busy chasing the bucks. After that, it usually dawns on us that money isn't all it takes to get a sense of fulfillment. It takes meaning.

The advantage of turning a hobby into a business is that you end up with the feeling that you're never working. In my case, for instance, I like to talk and write, so I think of the time I spend making lectures, teaching, or writing as leisure time. That's why I often say that my customers pay for me to have fun. Since these activities take up most of my time, I can even say that I stopped working to devote myself to my hobby. What do I do when I'm not talking or writing? Well, then I rest.

Businesses frequently originate from some passion, such as music or photography. Or it's the poet who has ten thousand poetry books printed and then goes out selling them to friends or relatives. You must surely have run away from one of these types.

While a surfer might have his business boosted by the wave of the moment, the poet probably won't be as lucky. The same passion that drives a hobby turned into a business might make the entrepreneurial hobbyist blind; it could make him believe that the whole world likes what he does, what he spends all he makes on. He commonly believes that others will also want to spend. That's when the hobby stops being a business and turns into a trap.

Some hobbies have too few enthusiasts to be transformed into lucrative businesses. For instance, a coin collector could think that opening up a shop for his hobby in a small town might be a good business. If that's your case, you'd better get ready to have a tough time explaining to your wife why, with so much money in the shop window, you can't afford to provide for your family.

Fanatic hobbyists who are insensitive to the needs and wants of people end up collecting businesses that are not very profitable. The enthusiast willing to turn his hobby into a business should first be perceptive enough to figure out if there are prospective clients for what he does. Sometimes there won't be, as in the case of a stamp collector, but his chances might improve if he expands the boundaries of his hobby. How so? I don't know, maybe opening a post office.

Therefore, even if a hobby has all it takes to become a business, that doesn't rule out the need for a good marketing plan. A good plan can help you determine start-up and maintenance costs, customer profiles, promotional techniques, delivery logistics, and many other variables that are important when undertaking any entrepreneurial venture. Be it a hobby or not.

Another thing the hobbyist bent on becoming a businessman should keep tuned to is overspending. Most people who are in love with a hobby tend to be liberal, recklessly spending with the excuse that they don't smoke, drink, or go out with friends. The hobbyist is a spendthrift who only thinks about the pleasure payoff. The entrepreneurial hobbyist, however, must be an investor, focusing on financial returns, on profits.

This is my tip: if you can't rein in your passion-turned-business, hire someone who can. It can be an administrator, an accountant or an honest partner If you prefer a tougher and more permanent control, get married.

MARIO PERSONA

New technologies

I f you can't manage to adapt to new technologies, it's going to be very difficult to change. You know who I'm talking about, the kind of person who faints in front of an ATM, checks the calculator results with a pencil and, when he phones to find out what time it is, he thanks the digital voice and even tries to make a pass at the girl. Worse than not adapting to new technologies, is resisting them and even trying to convince people that life was easier in the old days.

I used to resist technology, to the point that I dropped out of my architecture course in college to live in the woods. As a matter of fact, I moved to Alto Paraíso, a small village lost in the heart of Brazil. If you had met me there, you'd have called me a hippie, someone who escaped from civilization to live in the bush, raising goats, chickens and ticks. Your perception would be correct. My intention in those distant 70's was to save the world from the then-existing technology, but that didn't last long. I mean, the intention didn't, because the technology is still around.

You see, I didn't want to save the world from *all technology*, but only from the old-fashioned, dumb and polluting kind. Obviously, not everything in my mind was off-base, but every young guy has his chance to challenge the status quo with a crazy mix of illusion and reason in his attitudes.

At 23, after reaching the conclusion that everyone else was wrong, except myself, of course, I decided to roll up my sleeves and do something. I thought that with my pioneering example, I would be able to inspire the planet's population to use renewable resources and technology. You don't get it? I'll explain.

At the time, I was crazy about alternative and sustainable technologies, which I considered *"intelligent technology"*. Officially, I was in the bush to put into practice my projects regarding the protection of natural resources, research of low environmental impact technologies, and the earth's sustainable development. Unofficially, I wanted adventure, adrenaline, and an escape from my post-puberty responsibilities. Three years later I came back from the woods, still adept at "intelligent" conservation technology.

I was then forced into the computer age. I remember my fear when sitting in front of the first personal computer that I came across, without understanding the personal aspect of that experience. I trembled at the sight of those little green letters that appeared on that dark, mysterious screen. Could there have been a little man inside that box? When I went to work in a company where using one of the first Apple computers was mandatory, I took on an attitude of mockery. *That* was certainly a fad that wouldn't stick, I scoffed, trying to cover my fear of revealing my ignorance.

When I realized that there was no way out, that it was me or the machine, I decided it was time to tame it. With the excuse of it being a gift to my children, I bought an MSX computer, and spent nights trying to unravel its mysteries. I must confess that part of that time was spent destroying monsters and alien spaceships with my laser beam cannons, but I would rather this not be included in my biography.

Further on, my issues became virtual, and I sank into the wired world, to the point that people thought I was an expert on the subject. The Internet was still in diapers and I was already giving lectures, while still foreseeing very little of the potential of that new technology. Everything was new, everything would change, and everyone could make a buck, we thought. Well, the Internet bubble burst, and not everyone gained. I did. I gained experience.

With time, I learned to feel at home with the new technologies, and, nowadays, I don't avoid them anymore. Obviously I haven't mastered all of them. I still can't set my VCR clock, but with DVD and later cable TV, I didn't have to learn that.

I now live technologically connected in the comfort of my home-office, surrounded by devices created to make my life easier. Almost all my clients reach me via Internet; I would be just another has-been if it weren't for information technology. Of course, not everything is perfect. I get packages of spam and viruses along with my clients. Some I delete, others I exterminate. As for clients, I caress them with virtual proposals of real services.

Usually my clients only get to meet me face to face at the airport:

"I didn't even recognize you," they usually say. "You looked younger on the site's pictures..."

I explain to them that, on those pictures, I use *Photoshop Lotion for Wrinkles*.

I don't amount to much today, but without technology, I wouldn't amount to anything. I'd still be in the same time biomass of the hippie days, living on air without even having wind power generators to sell.. I even get the shivers when I come across some professional who keeps finding excuses not to use technology. I myself could come up with all sorts of excuses not to use the cell phone since I hate phone conversations, but I use it in order to do my job.

The same happens with the computer, a technology that my generation only got acquainted with in their 30's or 40's. Some haven't yet and are still living in the time that secretaries used to type memos. Do you believe that the other day I got an e-mail with those file reference numbers, like we used to have in office mail? I know this person, and I know she prints all the e-mails she receives, and sends and stores them in a filing cabinet.

Some time ago I met a friend of mine who is a consultant and told him how I developed my *modus operandi*. After I found out that none of my clients come to me — it's always the other way round — I closed my office, hired an answering service company and set up an office at home. From my home office, or my cell phone while I travel, I keep my business going and attend to my clients.

I don't know what my friend has decided to do since then, but when I told him how much I save working at home, he looked at me as if I were an alien from outer space. This guy has been keeping a rented place with a secretary just to answer the phone, not to mention that when she's pregnant, sick, or on vacation he has to hire somebody else to take her place. In all these years, not one of his clients has come to his office, but he only realized this after talking to me.

The problem of many professionals is that they have in mind the old model, where every business needs its own bricks and mortar headquarters, people commuting to work there, tables and a sign at the door. I know that for many firms this is vital, but it doesn't apply to all activities, especially for professionals dealing with knowledge, who are self-employed or associated. With a cell phone, notebook and the Internet, my office can be anywhere on the planet, and my signpost is on the Web.

That's the advice I've always given to my Business Administration students, in case they decide to work on their own, or set up their own business. First of all, I tell them that they should prefer some activity that does not require capital, employees, space, or stock. Impossible? That's the way I work. My capital is intellectual, I hire contractors when I need to, space is what I have on my hard drive, and stock is what I keep in between my ears.

Sure, if it's not possible to live in the best of worlds, then I suggest you look for something that doesn't require one or more of those items. A self-employed salesman or commercial representative, for instance, can work perfectly well using people, space, and stock from his supplier.

This is how I see it: if all the scientists that made the genome project a reality had to be in the same lab to do what they did, the project would never have taken off. Today the Internet is behind great achievements, whose work teams never met, and the same can happen to you.

Lack of adaptation to new times can cost those who resist their careers. That is why I advise people to start using the new technologies right away in order to decrease their efforts, bolster efficiency, and produce effective results. Use your muscles in the gym, not on the job; that's what I tell anyone who wants to know my opinion. Not everyone, however, follows my advice.

The hotel porter was one of them. I arrived at the lobby with a hefty suitcase crammed with the material that I was going to use in a time-management training. I was piloting the huge suitcase myself, thanks to the little wheels that gracefully glided across the floor.

But the young man didn't let me go on as he snatched the suitcase away from me. After all, he was the hotel porter and wanted to live up to the title by carrying my luggage, so much so that he grabbed it, as if performing the thirteenth labor of Hercules, exerting a superhuman effort to keep it at the level of his chest.

"It has little wheels... all you have to do is pull..." I suggested.

"I can handle it..." he groaned, all macho.

And he did, sweating and breathless through the corridors to the training room, where other people would learn to optimize work without wasting time or energy. He arrived embracing the suitcase, without letting it touch the floor in a heroic resistance to one of the oldest technologies: the wheel.

Opportunity

The clock strikes 2:45 AM and I've had an inspiration. Should I put it on paper? I have a notepad and pen on the bedside table, but this time I run to the computer. What happens if I don't write it down? I'll forget it. Besides, I get my best ideas in the morning, maybe because they reach the brain first without having to stand in line with the usual daily tasks and worries.

The thing works more or less like the biblical episode about the manna, when the Israelis wandered through the desert and were fed by the substance that fell from the sky at dawn and lay on the drew. The Israelis were told to collect the manna early in the morning, or it would melt, and vanish with the heat of the sun. Furthermore, manna from one day would be useless for the next; it could not be stored. It would have to be gathered again, every day, early in the morning.

That's what opportunities are like. They come and we have to take them right away, or they will dissipate or move on. You have to do something with them fast, use them somehow. In order not to let them go, I'm always paying attention to my senses, especially in the morning when my brain functions better. Perhaps it's another time for you, but the opportunities come just the same, merely waiting to be seized. You have to be ready for them, developing a kind of sixth sense to be able to recognize them and hear their murmurs.

Call it intuition, insight or inspiration, it is not enough just to have this feeling; it must be firmly connected to the opportunity. Or, if you prefer, you must have perfect timing. My dictionary defines timing as the "capacity to acknowledge the exact moment of doing something or perceiving the occurrence of something."

I began thinking about this concept two dawns ago, while I watched a documentary about the incredible Robert Allen Zimmerman (a good name for a Jewish jeweler, but not for someone like Bob Dylan, poet and singer). Introduced to the civil rights movement by Joan Baez, Dylan is the typical case of talent who became a success and grinned thanks to the timing of the wind. My goodness! I can't believe that I wrote this ridiculous rhyme! I think it's because "Blowing in the Wind" — adopted as the civil rights hymn in the 60's — is messing up my neurons this silent early morning.

But that's the way it was. Protesting against discrimination in the U.S.A. was the flavor of the month, and the poet savored the moment. It was the perfect timing to board the opportunity wagon, and he did so. Whether or not he was aware of it, everyone saw him traveling in the first class window. However, after the dust settled and Martin Luther King's body chilled, Dylan shocked his fans by electrifying his guitar and changing his speech. He changed his tune, less folk and more rock. *"...your old road is rapidly aging, please get out of the new one if you can't lend your hand, oh the times they are a changing"*.*

Dylan wasn't the only singer to profit from timing. At the time, there wasn't quite as much social activism in the United Kingdom as in the United States, but there was youth looking for alternatives. It was the right time for a *good-guys* band and a *bad-guys* band: the Beatles and the Rolling Stones.

Well, in the beginning they both were dressed like bad guys in leather and with unkempt hair, but Brian Epstein, a visionary and cunning businessman, decided to change the Beatles' image and present them as well-behaved, wearing suits and Chanel hairstyles. It was a hygienic alternative to the Rolling Stones and a way for dad and mum to allow their kids to go to the shows. Do you believe these things aren't intentional?

But times continued to change, and John Lennon became the Bob Dylan of the Beatles. When the time came, he cunningly perceived that it would be the perfect moment to wave the protest flag.

I know that there are going to be fans wanting to kill me as they did with him, but it seems pretty obvious that Lennon took advantage of the moment, literally stripping himself of western values and adopting, along with his wife, oriental values. Lennon put on the notoriety

---

* "The times they are changing" - Bob Dylan

hat when he posed nude in his rehearsed protest. But, without him, the rest of the band seemed naked. *"All you need is love..."* and timing.

A sense of opportunity is generally translated as luck by those who are always complaining that they don't have it and who envy those who do. You not only need to have it, but you must also know how to manage it. Opportunities do not come up to you with a neon light flashing "SEIZE ME!" or providing you with million-dollar results right away. Sometimes they only pass by, insinuating themselves or whispering something in the ears of your mind. They often show up along with some circumstances, preferably the ones that make us rise from the seat of indolence. The worse the circumstances, the more opportunities arise. Many of the great inventions that make our lives easier today sprung from times of war.

Some people think only great opportunities are worthwhile. Wrong. In much the same way as the invention of the computer, which was only possible thanks to thousands of small inventions, a big opportunity can be built with small ones that you seize throughout your life. An insignificant event in the short-term can have colossal long-term impacts. The big problem with opportunities is that they sometimes require us to break courtship with past ones — something that becomes increasingly difficult as we move on in years.

But no change takes place without someone getting hurt. At the end of the past century I only wrote and lectured about the Internet. That was the *"in"* thing then. As Bob Dylan fans complained when he changed, some of my readers — what a presumptuous comparison! — also complained when I shifted to writing about marketing, career management and so on. I lost some readers, while gaining others.

When the telephone first came out, someone who spoke about that new technology would have been able to attract a considerable audience. Today nobody would leave home to listen to a speaker expound on the wonders of the telephone! Whoever insists on always doing the same thing is going to be left behind by the speed of changes. So take note: if you don't manage your timing, people are going to forget about you.

Now that fans of Bob Dylan and John Lennon have probably sworn me to death, I might as well speak a little bit about the sense of opportunity of Bono Vox, pseudonym of Paul David Hewson. Like Bob Dylan and John Lennon in their day, Bono Vox has become an icon in the era of social inclusion. On top of being a talented artist, Bono Vox is a guy with a great sense of opportunity.

Note that having a sense of opportunity is not the same as being opportunistic, in a negative sense. Having a sense of opportunity is being intelligent; it's knowing how to link art to a cause, or cause to an art. It means satisfying the public in what's important for them. It's having both what's convenient and pleasant; it's being constantly on the move. Bono Vox does that. It is not enough to be good in what you do. You also have to know when to do it.

Many small-time artists fail to go on from the warm-up stage to bigger things, due only to lack of timing. This warm-up stage might also represent an opportunity as long as one does not stay in it forever. That's why there's something else I must include in this subject: A sense of opportunity stems from having both presence of mind and good communication skills. Bono Vox displayed these parallel qualities in an interview he gave before one of his shows in Brazil. The conversation went more or less like this:

Reporter: *"How do you feel about the fact that your show is taking place right after the one given by the Rolling Stones, which attracted more than a million people?"*

Bono Vox: *"I find it great! They warmed up the Brazilian public for our show!"*

He's just "bono de vox", "good of voice" and a witty artist of conversation.

Personal marketing

Narcissus was a young Greek whose iPod was his mirror; he wouldn't let go of it. As for his neighbor, Agnes Gonxha Bojaxhiu, she didn't have an iPod. Instead, for most of her life, she listened to the moaning of the old people, the blind, and the lepers of Calcutta, who called her Mother Teresa. What did she and Narcissus have in common? Personal marketing. Both of them became known all over the world without spending one drachma or one rupee on propaganda.

According to the *Google Analytics*, which monitors my website, 91% of the people who visit it do so via links from other sites or search engines. The former are links created by those who visited me online and liked what I wrote, or by those who publish the texts that I hand out as free offers. For some years, I have been writing a weekly column about life, career, and business in my blog and the texts are also sent to thousands of subscribers to my electronic bulletin, who can also publish them as collaboration in their blogs, newspapers, magazines and websites.

I also write texts exclusively for corporate magazines, which I get paid for, but the texts I publish in my blog and give out free are part of a strategy I took on some years back, aiming to expand the scope of my texts and to obtain a good position in search sites. These usually decide which pages to show first in search results based on the number of links from other sites directed to those pages. Therefore, the more people point to my site, the better my position will be in the search sites' ranking.

I also saw on *Google Analytics* that the expression which directs more people to my site is *personal marketing*. It is interesting to note how this subject has attracted people's attention. Maybe it's because of the increasing number of professionals who have gone from a traditional job to a solo career of service provider. When you have to sell your own talent, it is vital to develop a good personal marketing strategy.

But what is personal marketing? Personal marketing means identifying people's needs and desires, and attending to them. Contrary to what many believe, personal marketing isn't self-promotion. Even though promotion is taught at marketing schools as being one of the elements of marketing, in the case of personal marketing, promotion isn't done by you, the most interested party, but by others.

To understand this better, the focus in personal marketing starts with the product. The product is yourself, but not in a narcissistic sense. There's no point in trying to gain your market and being remembered by people, if you don't have a good product — if you don't have talent and competence to do what you do. If your "product" isn't good, you might even be remembered, but not the way you'd like to be. In order to have a successful product, your assembly line should have started way back, in your upbringing, character and education. If it didn't, you can still take on corrective actions, in case you're tired of being rejected due to one or more *non-conformities*.

Non-conformities arise when a *quality control audit* spots *benchmarking variations* in *performance* that prevent the identification of your *capability* or acceptable *stability rate* in *statistics process control* results that meet *client specifications* or *requirements*, after a *ppm* or *parts per million* analysis.

Never mind the *gobbledegook*. This paragraph is just to rattle on with words that tend to impress corporate people more concerned about the quality of screws than the quality of the people who produce them. Ah! Let's add another one: *ISO 9000*, so this may be found in case someone looks it up in Google.

While we're on the subject of Google, the world is like a huge search engine, where we can be found by the words and actions we leave behind. Everything we do in the real world ends up being recorded in someone's memory, in much the same way as everything we publish in the virtual world is registered in easy-to-find places, but is impossible to delete.

I remember a young man who, a few years back, hacked an e-mail discussion group, of which I was the moderator. Using digital tracking techniques and social engineering, I followed his footsteps until I had his name, address and even the company he worked for. Obviously, this all ended up being discussed in countless e-mail messages exchanged in that debate forum.

Much later he wrote me, asking me to erase the texts that discussed his invasion from the forum, because they showed up whenever anyone looked up his name in the Web. At the time, I couldn't do anything for I no longer had access to the server where the messages remained indefinitely. For some years, his name will continue to bear that negative reputation, and he'll be unable to gather up all the feathers that were scattered by the winds of the virtual world.

I also met a Brazilian consultant who, upon realizing that cooperating with free articles in other people's sites was a good strategy to become well-known, started to do the same. The problem was that, due to a lack of talent or time, he translated articles from American authors and published them in Portuguese, as if they were his own. One of his readers thought he had already read one of his articles in English, so he decided to check. He translated a sentence from the article into English and did a Google search. When he found the real author and unveiled the consultant's fraud, he did the same to other articles and then leaked the scam to thousands of people in discussion forums where the consultant was known.

Personal marketing is, therefore, a marketing of consequences, where we reap what we sow. What makes it different from corporate or product marketing is that in the case of the latter you can simply close up shop and open another, or change the soap brand, if things go wrong. "Soap X" leaves spots? No problem, we trade it for "Soap Y" with a new formula. Change the brand, the name, the package and most people won't bother finding out who the manufacturer is.

The same can't be done where you as a person are concerned. You can't be replaced by someone else, or have your name or package replaced. You will continue being you even if you move to another town. The memory of what you were or did will remain alive for years to come, thanks to the indelible mark you left. How many years? Well, you've probably heard about Adam and what he did, haven't you? That was quite some time ago.

Thus the importance of a personal marketing approach focusing on you, your integrity, your attitudes, principles, your... everything! Every action causes a reaction, good or bad. That's what I told a journalist at the end of an interview:

> "The golden rule is to do to others what you would like them to do to you. The strategy seeks to expand the network of people who might recommend you. When we realize that 'brand' is the mark we leave on others — be it positive or negative — we start taking better care of our personal marketing, more in the likes of Mother Teresa than Narcissus."

Where was this quote published? In the 30-year issue of TAM Magazine, the flight magazine of Brazil's largest airline. That's right, TAM, founded by Commander Rolim, who used to stand by the plane door greeting and talking to passengers boarding the plane. Years after his death, he is still remembered for what he did, and for the red carpet he actually rolled out to welcome his clients as they boarded. What he did, and the impression he left behind, is personal marketing.

Networking

Want some advice? Invest and insist on networking. The word networking is closely tied to the timeless concept of friends and relationships, from the neighborly days when people used to take chairs to the sidewalk, or gossip leaning on broomsticks during housework breaks. Well, the chairs have gone back to the kitchen, people are stuck in front of computers, videos, and TVs, and in the age of vacuum cleaners, broomsticks only show up at Halloween parties.

Technology brought us the vacuum cleaner; it also brought us a new contact and gossip tool: the Internet, with its chat rooms, forums and virtual communities. In much the same way as in the real world where you hire on recommendation, the same happens in the virtual world. Nowadays even HR professionals access relationship communities to find out about the personal lives of those they wish to hire. The police do the same to find out about people they arrest.

Take a deep breath and you'll experience the importance of networking, the extent of your contact network, and the capillarity you should create in the market. Our lungs have the largest surface of our bodies in contact with the atmosphere: almost 80 square meters of alveoli. Life would be impossible if it weren't for this constant exchange of gases with the environment. I'm not suggesting that you just keep exchanging gases with the atmosphere. My point is that, just as your lungs do, you should have a wide surface of exposure and capillarity, or networking, in order to be found, help, and be helped.

In the virtual world, though, investing in exposure isn't enough. One needs wisdom and perceptiveness when being exposed. The advantage of the virtual is even greater for people like me, who, in the real world, are ill-suited for parties, dinners, and bar tables. I know there are lots of people like that, people with few friends, who only practice individual sports and avoid parties and crowds, keeping a low profile.

Are you like that? That makes two of us. It's true, I am an introvert. You might not think so, but I prefer rainy days to sunny ones, and I only call people when I have to. I never ever chat on the phone. I hate receiving or making phone calls. Those who call me think that I am unfriendly, that I'm saving words, because the conversation turns into a monologue, theirs. That doesn't mean I'm some kind of Steppenwolf, detached from everything and everyone. Much to the contrary.

Because of my disposition, I ended up creating a huge network of virtual relationships, people I've been in touch with for years, without ever having felt their breath. It was from this network of mine that I received the news that my fifth book *"People Marketing"* was ranked fifth on the bestseller list in its category of a major bookstore in Brazil. Philip Kotler was fourth. But there's more to my relationship network.

While my national network informed me that *"Você S.A"* magazine mentioned another book of mine on one of its pages, my international one revealed that a text from my book *"Great Business Recipes"* adorned the back of the menu of a Brazilian restaurant in Miami. It wasn't the same text that had been plagiarized by some half dozen pseudo-writers, something else I later learned from my network. It was also through my virtual network, and from people who only knew me through Facebook, MySpace, Orkut or other communities, that I closed deals with excellent clients. What about your network, what has it done for you?

Relationship networks have always existed, but now technology has broadened their scope. If you know how to take advantage of them, you have a lot to gain. That's what a Brazilian company did to poll their extra-strong mint consumers, the kind I use in my lectures. How do I know this? Someone from my virtual network told me. After ruling out conventional means of research, due to the difficulty of rapidly gathering a population of mint consumers, the company decided to break ground and go to Orkut.

That's where they found all kinds of mint-lovers communities, where people talked without smelling each other's breath and were more than willing to talk about their preferences. This precedent, polling where people are already united by affinity, could change a lot of things. Obviously, the company didn't tell its client how easy it had been to do a poll that a few years back would have required research teams all over town.

The other day, someone who was looking over my shoulder while I read messages in my Orkut profile, uttered a harsh and dry remark: *"This thing's good for the ego"*. That may be true for most people, but for me it's been good for my wallet. Letting on, in relationship sites, discussion groups and even in YouTube videos, a little bit of what you are and what you can do means potential profits.

If, on the one hand, technology has established a certain distance between people, on the other hand it can be used to create some intimacy, so my clients can realize that I am a human being, with emotions and features that would otherwise be practically impossible to pass on without a personal contact.

Like everything else in life, there's a flipside, and great care must be taken when you expose yourself. Businesses, marriages, crimes — they can all be found in the virtual environment — just like in real life. Although the environment is virtual, the elements that make it up are still real people. There are advantages, but also dangers, that's inevitable. But it's a new way of getting in touch, with previously unimaginable benefits, this no one can deny.

We all know, of course, that nothing can replace live contact, talking face-to-face and eye-to-eye. Just as you have to take certain precautions when establishing virtual contacts, the same goes for personal relationships. Especially if you're dealing with someone who twitches and has strange habits.

I mean the guy who holds your hand from beginning to end of a conversation. You must know someone like that. Please don't tell anyone I mentioned him here, but he sure is a pain in the neck. If his hands are wet and sticky, then you'll regret you didn't send an e-mail.

There's also the one who speaks really close to you, and doesn't even remember to chew some mint tablets. You know, the kind who gets all over you, shadowing you wherever you go. You must also know this type. Don't even hint that I mentioned him here.

And what about the one who likes to poke your belly? Now, that's one big hassle if you're ticklish or have a belly-button hernia. An even stranger habit is that of those who like to fiddle with your shirt buttons while they talk. I met someone who did just that when talking to me. It must have been some kind of insecurity, a need to keep his finger on some button to feel connected. People like that must see a keyboard in every belly in front of them, and can't talk without pretending they're typing. Are you like that?

If you are, let me ask you this: do you do it to feel safe, to narrow the gap that sets you apart from other people, to reach out. . or what exactly? I've always wanted to ask. What do people like you do when they come across someone in a T-shirt? And before the zipper was invented, how would they proceed when talking to someone wearing a T-shirt and buttoned pants? You want some advice? Stick to pushing your own buttons.

Creativity

What is this, what is that?
It's a table, it's a chair;
What is that Mister Payne?
It's a big airplane.
What is that, what is this?
It's a book, it's a kiss;
What is that silver chain?
It's a subway train.

It was by singing these verses that I started my English lessons in the small town of Alto Paraíso, in central Brazil. The year? 1979. Why was I there? To change the world. That's what I had set out to do when I was 23 years old, less than half what I am now. My private humanitarian project made me put my architecture degree on ice, and move, dad-sponsored, to the country in a van packed with junk and dreams. There I learned that the world is too big to be changed and that the best strategy is to start with people, even if they seem bigger than the world.

My first challenge was to make those kids learn to speak English in a place with no phones or TV signals. Besides that I taught them math and science, and pretended to discuss a subject called Political and Social Organization of Brazil, at a time when the military dictatorship banned any real discussion of the issue. That wrapped up the discipline package I was assigned, after it was handed out among the few citizens willing to educate and prepare those rustic minds for the crazy world they would face. That is, if Skylab didn't fall over their heads, a constant concern voiced via the short-wave radio transmissions that reached the place.

I took up my own audiovisual method — I sang to the sound of my twelve string guitar, as two dozen eyes watched me sway. That's what I started doing when I realized that nothing in that remote part of the world in which they lived would convince them that they should learn English. I don't know if they did learn, but I could bet that even today, there must be some dad or mom out there singing *"What is this, what is that?"* to put their children to sleep.

The secret to getting the message across was in the ingredients that I unconsciously used in that improvised method: idealism, good spirits, audacity, and passion. The sound that vibrated in the classroom atmosphere had the effect of overcoming barriers and stimulating their appetite for new things. Yes, they sang along. And how!

Only much later would I learn the power of creativity in demolishing feuds of psychological resistance forged by traditional education. Pablo Picasso used to say that every creation starts with an act of destruction, but it is the teacher played by Robin Williams in *"Dead Poet's Society"* who paints this in color on canvas. In the film, the students of *Welton Academy* are encouraged to rip a conservative essay out of their textbooks and stand on the teacher's table as a reminder to look at the world in a different way.

In an e-book titled *"Sly as a Fox,"* Mark L. Fox, who must be related to the title, informs us that the creativity of a child, from ages 5 to 7, drops 90%. At age 40, one's creativity is only 2% of what it initially was. It doesn't matter if he said that based on some scientific research or on his own creativity. What matters is that conventional education clogs our creative capacity by over-stimulating rational thought.

In school we learn that knowing how to answer is more important than knowing how to ask, that making mistakes is wrong and not part of the learning process, and that those who copy don't learn. The library teaches us that study is something that should be done alone, that concentration is the most important thing and that interruptions are most annoying. The University would have us believe that we should become specialists, that those who write well get the highest grades, and that accuracy is the goddess of education. Only later, much later, do we learn that things are not always like that outside the academic ivory tower.

A reporter, when interviewing Thomas Edison, inquired if it was true that he had tried and failed a certain number of times before discovering the right filament for his lamp. Edison replied that he hadn't failed; rather, he had invented a certain number of ways of not making a lamp. Don't ask me how many times, because in the hundreds of times that Google points to this story, the number ranges from an exact 1346 to a generic 9999. While we're on the subject of creativity, just remember the story and put precision aside, because, after leaving school, we won't be dealing with a world of precise facts, but with an ocean of ambiguities.

Outside academic walls, we find that we need to be enough of a generalist in order to survive changes and that it is not the one who writes better that succeeds, but the one that speaks better. Or the one who copies. Wait, don't tear your hair out yet. I don't mean *copy-paste*, but copy that improves on what was created in order to create something new.

In a scene from the movie *"Finding Forrester,"* the one in which *"James Bond"* receives the tricky mission of becoming a writer, *Sean-Forrester-Bond-Connery* teaches his student to escape from the prison that terrifies every writer: the blank page. He tells the boy to copy the first paragraph of a text, just to stimulate his brain. From then on, *Chip and Dale* (the Walt Disney chipmunks that I will adopt to characterize the two residents inside our skulls) discover their own way to an all-original adventure. From that point, the writing flows naturally.

Both of them, Chip and Dale, work on results, but Chip isn't the creative one. Chip's a lawyer who lives in the left hemisphere of our brain, and takes care of everything that's rational. He is addicted to order, analytical thinking and literality. His TV set is black and white, his drafts are underlined with a ruler, he hates interruptions, and he doesn't deviate from his schedule for anything in the world.

Chip, the lawyer, would never see, in the letters of the word *America*, the name *Iracema*, given by the Brazilian writer José de Alencar to the main character of his novel with the same name. In his book *Iracema* is the innocent virgin native woman who represents the original America. For the rational Chip, everything can only be one thing: what it is. And it can have only one explanation: the one that explains. He hates ambiguities, delays, and imperfections. He is the type who reads the manual every night, before going to bed with his beloved female chipmunk.

In the burrow next door — on the right hemisphere — lives Dale, the artist. He unveils the context of everything, lives in a state of emotion, and is skilled at synthesizing any thing or situation. Dale, the artist, isn't tied to standards nor does he have a conventional TV. What he has is a bubble, in which he floats while he watches everything from his swivel armchair in a multidimensional polyphonic sound screen. Dale is intuitive and does more than one thing at the same time, all new things. He doesn't have a timetable or an agenda, and he sees interruptions as opportunities.

Dale, the artist, has only one problem. Everything he does or creates only leaves the neurological tree after being inspected by Chip, the lawyer. This inspection is the filter that turns Dale's creation into intelligible communication for the other Chips and Dales that inhabit the human forest. Too much creativity ends up being filtered by rationality, where there is no place for daydreaming or inaccuracy. The lawyer Chip doesn't use a color printer. His paws interpret what Dale says on an old typewriter.

The same happens in the opposite direction. All the information that reaches our brain chipmunks' tree must first go through the lawyer Chip. He checks everything, sitting at his desk, illuminated by the lamp of rationality, before sending what's left — not much — in fact, to our memory files. In the meantime, Dale, the artist, listens to music, is delighted by poetry and works of art, things that mean nothing to Chip. That's where the dribbling technique comes in.

I'll explain. If you listen to your girlfriend talking about her love for you, you sigh. If she whispers a poem in your ears with a sweet voice, you shiver. Then all your strength vanishes away, sucked into invisible drains, when you see those eye colors that range from petrol to sky melting with passion. You stop caring if the shape of her face is oval like a circle, if the body you embrace is less than perfect, if her vocabulary is as limited as... hmmm... well, forget it. Everything is delightful, touching... It's all fabulous until she pops the question, "Let's get married?" That's when you turn things over to Chip, your lawyer in the rational department.

Before lawyer Chip came into the picture, the effect of that poetic moment was the same as the one caused by the twelve strings of my guitar in the minds of my students. In a class that was used to the rough country life and to a lack of prospects of moving away from it, there was nothing logical or rational about learning English. Chip the lawyer living in the minds would dismiss any attempt of learning a foreign language as absolutely illogical. Why would anyone who lives among cows, horses and chickens need to speak English? That's where I would dribble in the rational, with creativity, art and emotion.

Everything that comes to us in the form of art, rhyme and beat enters next door from the rational scrutiny. The brain identifies them as things we shouldn't interpret, but enjoy. In communication, the ability of seasoning your message with the sauce of artistic creativity has the power of softening the rationality concrete, and liberating abstract emotion. Once settled in the comforting corner of Dale's liberal burrow, the message can generate naughty little chipmunks, that, every now and then, will run away to spread their hazelnuts to the most out-of-the-way cubbyholes of the forest. And they'll germinate.

In his book *"A Whole New Mind – Moving from the Information Age to the Conceptual Age"*, Dan Pink writes: *"The era of the supremacy of the 'left hemisphere' – and the Information Era that it created – is giving way to a new world where the qualities of the 'right hemisphere' – creativity, empathy, meaning – will prevail."* And he concludes: *"The MFA,"* or Master of Fine Arts, *"is the new MBA,"* on pointing to a world where people will increasingly look for concepts, experiences and meanings in things.

Knowledge that can be explained on paper, or reasoning that can be processed digitally, will quickly become a commodity. What will then have value is what cannot be explained, replicated, or artificially produced: creativity. Just as machines substituted for raw strength in the past, computers can replace a great deal of present logical thought, increasing the value of things like beauty, introspection and emotion. These are things that are not rational; rather, the rational things exist to serve them.

I obviously didn't know all this in my youth, when I sang and danced without worries to my two dozen students, with my twelve string guitar tied to a colored strap hanging from my neck.

> *What is that, what is this?*
> *It's a book, it's a kiss;*
> *What is that silver chain?*
> *It's a subway train.*

But there I understood that not everything could be just fun and games, and that Chip and Dale would have to work as partners if there was to be any operational creativity. I realized that when a student asked:

"Teacher, what's a subway train?"

I explained that a subway train is the same as a metro, a train that travels through underground tunnels. In the silence that followed it was evident that something was missing. Then a female student, bold and sincere, raised her hand. Her question made me realize how much groundwork I would still have to do on those minds that had never ventured beyond the remote town of Alto Paraíso.

"Teacher, what is a train?"

Ambiguity

D id Adam have a navel? That depends. Considering he wasn't born of a woman, the answer could
be no. However, taking into account that he was
created as a full-fledged adult prototype, then it could
be yes. It's that simple. But some people have difficulty
dealing with ambiguous situations such as this one.

The dictionary defines "ambiguous" as something that
raises doubt, uncertainty, something vague, obscure,
indefinite, prone to multiple interpretations, and even
having opposite meanings. It's a thing or situation that
can be seen from varying angles, leading to conflicting
conclusions and answers that might not be yes or no,
much to the contrary. Get it? You don't have to, because
it might all be the other way round.

The world we live in is a mass of ambiguities, where not
everything can be controlled, as Max Weber, a lover of

bureaucracy as an efficient organization system, would have liked. If you add to ambiguity the ever-changing nature of living and working conditions, it would be perfectly normal to feel utterly at a loss in this world. Everything is uncertain, unpredictable; it all turns out to be what we didn't expect. If you want your career to survive, you'll have to learn to make decisions in this unstable environment. Do you agree? If you don't, that's just fine.

There is, however, a brighter side to ambiguity. As children, we pretended to see lambs in clouds. We spent hours discovering a world of voluptuous shapes that could be anything our imagination wanted. Even so, it wasn't a static scenario, for the action of the wind forced us to reconstruct our analogies each second.

But we started school, and in the gray, rational classroom we were taught that all of that was no more than a visible set of water particles suspended in the atmosphere. There, it was all explained. We could go back to our times table, patriotic dates, and equations. And God help anyone who said that one plus one was eleven or that the pens we tossed around were spaceships. A pen was a pen, air was air, and a spaceship was a spaceship. Nothing could have more than one explanation, meaning or reason.

Hitler was one who had great difficulty dealing with ambiguity. For him, nothing could be less than perfect, his way. In order to have things the way he wanted, he eliminated imperfections the hard way. In Nazi architecture, it was enough to include a window on the left façade, symmetrical to the window on the right, and everything would be beautiful and perfect. Or simply eliminate the windows that did not fit the previously established standards, or even the people who dared to look through them, as he seemed to prefer.

The same logic applied to art during that era. Unable to eliminate the clouds, he exterminated those who painted them and those who wrote or made films that were subject to more than one interpretation. Hitler tried to do the same to human imperfections; he wanted to get rid of everything that wasn't perfectly standardized and spinning in the mandatory direction of his swastika.

To create his perfect and predictable world, it was necessary to eliminate anything circumstantial. But it was precisely the circumstances that prevented him from perfecting his plan. On circumstances, Aristotle said, "It's probable that the improbable will occur." That's also very true of careers and businesses.

Knowing how to work in environments of uncertainty and ambiguity is vital for any career. If you are one of those who waste a considerable amount of time making five or ten-year plans or forecasts straight-jacketed in accordance with what happened in the last decade, you'd better get used to the fact that nothing is 100% predictable or 100% controllable.

In every sure bet, there is a risk factor, and every rule has exceptions. We have never needed intuition, flexibility, and creativity as much as we do now. Why do you think women get along well with ambiguity? They have more intuition. But one of their qualities that are best suited for today's demands is their incredible capacity to deal with several things at the same time. Try taking care of half a dozen small children and you'll see there's no room left for certainty, predictability or reason.

We should adapt to circumstances we cannot change and manage the ones we think we can. I think I copied this from Reinhold Niebuhr's Serenity Prayer: *"God, give us grace to accept with serenity the things that cannot be changed, courage to change the things that should be changed, and the wisdom to distinguish the one from the other."* This prayer was adopted by Alcoholics Anonymous, whose members practice the philosophy of *"one day at a time."* In your job or career, this must be practiced with the right tools in order to deal with ambiguities and an unfavorable organizational environment.

In my trainings and workshops, I often stimulate creative thinking and tolerance to ambiguity in environments of uncertainty and risk, but I'm not always successful. Some people just can't see one palm — 9 inches to be exact — beyond the ingrained standards of their narrow minds. That's what I noticed when I used a scene from a Hollywood movie, to discuss its analogy with marketing and sales, in a workshop for engineers.

The scene from *"Schindler's List"* showed the character in a bar, trying to captivate his future market, Nazi officers. In the film, Schindler gives generous bribes to the waiter in order to move the dancers closer to the low-ranking officers, and to serve good wine to the high-ranking ones. My purpose was to show that we should identify and meet the needs and desires of customers, which, in that case, were money, pleasure, and prestige. It was my light version of Maslow's hierarchy of needs. When I finished presenting the scene, one of the participants raised his hand.

"I don't agree that you have to bribe someone, foster prostitution, or inebriate the client in order to sell," he said firmly.

I waited for him to criticize the scene's Nazi environment, but it seemed that he had nothing against that.

I was horrified at the thought of how he and others could be interpreting the analogy I was trying to get across. Apparently he was unable to deal with analogies, parables, and metaphors, or envisage more than one meaning or use for an idea, an object, or a situation.

People who never played the game of seeing lambs on clouds think only with the left hemisphere of rationality and believe that, in life, everything is black or white. They reckon that in order for something to exist, it must be concrete and its existence must be proven, tested, and bear the seal of approval from a duly certified laboratory, accompanied by dozens of graphics and charts. These are people who would only believe in Adam if one day *Discovery Channel* showed a navel-less human being in some museum.

I immediately remembered another workshop I had conducted a few days before, and I froze! That's because, to teach strategic thought, I used as an analogy a battle scene from the film *"Braveheart."* In this scene Mel Gibson, playing William Wallace, leads an army that chops off enemy legs, arms, and heads with swirling axes.

Why did I worry? Because my workshops focus on changing people's behavior, starting with leadership, and, if people take my analogies literally, I'll see newspaper headlines screaming:

"MANAGER PROMOTES CORPORATE BLOODBATH."

I dread the thought. I'll be arrested for masterminding the felony. Me and Mel Gibson.

Communication

The red light penetrated the makeshift stage, engulfing a slice of the darkness. Its focus revealed an old TV set, or what was left of one. Bought in a spare electronic parts shop, the huge wooden structure that had fed three generations of termites no longer had a kinescope or tubes. The box was hollow and empty, much like my own head at the time. Behind its brittle plastic screen, my painted face showed up to a surprised audience. The rest of my body was hidden in a cavity below the stage, under the TV box. I was squirming, as if desperate to escape the little screen, where everyone wanted to enter.

The stage and the audience belonged to the college where I was an architecture freshman. The mad show was our way of presenting a communication assignment that spoke out against the negative impact of the yellow press in society. Instead of handing in a bulky mass of typed pages, we decided to deliver some I-don't-know-what-kind-of-play, that was supposed to clarify (I don't know how) what its purposes were. It was something undefined even for us, the producers. We had created a rather impromptu performance that had only been rehearsed in the minds of each one of us.

At the time, the Kiss band was making it big with their exotic, flamboyant, plumy image, so we decided to take advantage of the moment. Being theatrical beginners, we painted each other with school paint, not foreseeing how uncomfortable that would feel after the paint dried up. The horrible faces we made, tortured by the itching and stinging from the dry paint under the spotlights, added a dramatic touch to our appearance.

From inside the TV box, I punched the plastic screen a little too hard, and came out of the hole to the next step, tearing the box apart in a mad rage, mimicking what some rock stars did to their guitars. This was being done to the sound of Rick Wakeman booming out of giant sound boxes to an audience at a loss as to whether we were just kidding or were supposed to be taken seriously. After me, my fellow thespians came onstage, each performing the scenes they had chosen for themselves.

One of them twisted a newspaper, spilling fake blood made of red ink, hidden in sponges squeezed between its pages. The other one made gestures behind a translucid panel made of stretched newspaper pages illuminated from behind to create a shadow theater effect. He pretended to have his pants down and, dropping newspaper balls into a bucket, he simulated the act of defecating. The contents of the bucket were then suddenly thrown to the astonished audience. With wild gestures, dances, leaps and screams, we did all we could to uphold the public's expectation that we had a message to convey, but we ourselves didn't know what our message was! At that point, my group and I were already regretting what we had done, admitting we had made an awful choice with that kind of communication and expression.

The fact of the matter is that, if anyone had asked, we wouldn't even have been able to give a definition of communication. No one had yet taught us that communication is thought turned into a message aimed at generating an action in its receiver, for a desired purpose. In a way, our communication, up until then, had managed to leave the audience astonished and actionless. We were far from believing that we could reach our desired goal, a good grade given by the teacher who watched it all from the first row.

But consider this: all actions, all endeavors, all accomplishments, large or small, begin with communication. Wars start and end with words. Even if you don't need to start or end wars, the principle remains valid, be it for a school assignment or for obtaining positive career results. But merely streamlining one's communication isn't enough; it must be given an original quality, a flavor no one else can give. One needs to add expression.

We were sure of having achieved that, thanks to the originality of the dry paint on our faces, which was already beginning to peel off. Even if we remained silent and static, our bodies would continue conveying visual messages. Yes, we transmit silent messages all the time, with our clothes, expressions, tone of voice, cell phone model, haircut, car — everything about us communicates through messages — positive and negative ones. We commonly come across people who say one thing but convey something completely different through their outward appearance. They're having a communication problem.

Our body is a movie with no admission fee for those willing to watch. The other day I was watching an executive in line at the airport. The employees were having difficulty operating the x-ray equipment and the line kept growing. He was right in front of me. I noticed his neck turning red below his ears. Then his arms started opening up as if he were carrying books under his armpits, somewhat suggestive of a rooster preparing to fight.

Then he placed his hands on his waist, sucked in his belly, puffed up his chest, and put one foot in front of the other, pointing the former to the employees, and keeping the latter in a transverse position, as if to ensure support. His posture was one of outrage and hostility; he seemed like an animal ready to attack. He didn't say a word, but his body was a speech and an unmistakable complaint box. A big one.

Learning to figure out the signs our bodies convey can be very helpful to professionals. Knowing how to interpret the inverse, that is, the signals you receive, also affect the back-and-forth of communication, sending and receiving messages continuously, verbal or non-verbal. One needs a good grasp of this in order to know how to handle the messages one sends, as well as recognizing and filtering the ones you receive.

Since effective communication depends on the public's correct understanding of it, it's also a continuous learning process in which the generation and emission of a message is as important as the evaluation of its feedback. Your target should be attaining a degree of clarity that allows you to send only the indispensable elements to a public who has no time to lose with a wearisome and complicated communication style. Brevity and simplicity prevail in modern communication. So do originality and creativity.

Having something to say isn't enough. One needs to capture the attention of a population diverted by tons of sensorial stimuli, continuously unloaded on its already bloated senses. Therefore, if you want to communicate well, to interact with people and influence them, you must first know what they're interested in, how they would like to be influenced, and the best way of interacting with them in order to get their attention.

That's one thing my buddies and I were sure of during our college presentation. We were certain of having captured the attention of the teacher and that of our student audience, but we had no idea what the result of that communication would be. The fact is we didn't even know if we had anything to communicate, apart from that crazy performance that used up a lot of newspapers to give the idea that our project was about the press and communication.

When the lights went on, we noticed that some people in the audience seemed to be balancing exclamation marks on their heads, while others were doing the same with question marks. Just like them, we had no idea what the whole thing meant. We expected the worst.

The teacher seemed flabbergasted. She admitted having no words to express herself, and stuttered an *"Excellent!"* It was the go-ahead sign for the applause to burst out. And it did, when the students realized that applause didn't mean consorting with the absurd. And the teacher, who expected just another typed up little homework, was surprised. We realized she was crazier than any of us.

Even so, she asked for a written interpretation of all that, just for the record. That's when we were surprised. One of us had the bright idea of asking if the typed and bound report could be handed in the following day. She agreed.

Then she, who at first had no words to express herself, began to speak. And how! She spoke about the meaning of our show, explaining every detail, every motion, every scream, and every drop of sweat. Even the paint masks gained a significance we ignored. While she spoke, someone in the group was taking notes. The next day we handed in the text, duly typed and getting the top grade. By an incredible coincidence, our explanation of the play was exactly the same as the teacher's.

That's when I learned the meaning of David Ogilvy' maxim:

"Communication isn't what you say; it's what the others understand."

Outsourcing

The ditch overflowed. Anyone who's gone through this knows what that means. The old ditch of the old house where I lived when I was still young had reached its limit. I urgently needed to find someone to dig a new one. I think people used to call these professionals *ditch-diggers*, but I didn't ever need to call one. A neighbor did that for me because the bad smell was becoming unbearable.

I wasn't impressed with the tall, skinny guy leaning on a shovel and cutting up tobacco with a penknife on the palm of his uncalloused hand. While he was preparing his cigarette, I started getting ready to go to work. Before leaving, I noticed the man was still in the same place, leaning on the same shovel, with the same little cigarette between his lips. But he was the only one standing still. The job was being done, but somebody else was digging.

He smiled at me, an almost-toothless yellow smile, and he explained, savoring words to the utmost:

"I outsourced."

Outsourcing is what mankind has been doing right from the beginning. In fact, we work with only one thing in mind: to stop working. That's right. The goal of working has always been leisure, the dream of retirement. Those who play the lottery are seeking a shortcut to a whole life of weekends, of Saturdays and Sundays, with no Mondays in sight. By inventing outsourcing, we created productive procrastination, the dream of all those eager to pass the buck.

Many people, despite knowing and hoping for this, have a hard time delegating work and responsibilities. These are people who get overburdened, who want to be everything to everyone, and perform tasks that anyone substituting them could take care of. They may have learned to conjugate every verb, except for the most important one: *I outsource, you outsource, he works*.

Let's go back to our history. First, we outsourced arm work to bludgeons, levers and tool handles, which were stronger and more efficient. Then we outsourced legwork, inventing the wheel. And that was just the beginning. The natural evolution of this outsourcing was traction, when we let the animals take care of heavy loads. Then things became more sophisticated, with sails taking advantage of wind power, watermills using water, and steam machines making the world go round. This has evolved in such a way that life would be impracticable without outsourced energy.

While the outsourcing of heavy work was in progress, we were outsourcing our senses too. We hired the ears of dogs to improve our hearing when watching over caves. Their eyes and snouts were also employed to see and sniff far better than any of us could. Before I forget, their teeth were also included in the property security and personal defense package. Once we had guard-dogs, we could already sleep peacefully, but we didn't want to miss waking up either. So we started raising roosters to wake us up at the right time and, long before e-mail was invented, we had pigeons flying around with our messages.

We continue our outsourcing saga with the production of food and clothing, taking on the cow to turn grass into protein, the ox to supply raw materials for combs, paintbrushes and shoes, and the bee to make honey from flowers. We didn't even spare bacteria in this widespread and unrestricted outsourcing process. They were hired to make bread grow, battle infection, and turn grapes and barley into happiness. We could toast to the working hours that we saved in our quest for idleness and leisure.

The great thing about outsourcing was the possibility of having time left over for nobler tasks such as thinking, painting, writing or singing. Without outsourcing, mankind would have never had time to develop other things that could be outsourced.

But outsourcing wasn't enough. Things had to be perfected, as we did with the dog. From only one ancestral mold, we created a dog for each profession: shepherds, guides of the blind, watchdogs, and the Saint-Bernard who serves mountain-climbers on the rocks. Some breeds, like old ladies' dogs, are absolutely useless, but they have learned fast to outsource; they have everything done for them by their owners.

When we reached our current state of development, we saw companies outsourcing their stock to suppliers, demanding on-time deliveries, and hiring outside services from third parties, who would, in turn, hire from fourth, fifth and sixth parties. Supermarkets, banks, phone companies and restaurants have been outsourcing customer services to their own clients, who are now waited on by themselves and so cannot complain. Now you, the customer, are the shop assistant, who takes the merchandise from the shelves and bags it; you're the bank clerk, who keys in numbers and prints receipts; you're the phone operator, making your own long-distance calls, and you're also the waiter of the self-service restaurant, carrying the tray. In the meantime, you outsource your messages to the answering machine, your diet to diet foods, and your abdominal crunches to a vibrating belt advertised on TV.

In this kind of economy, those who can't outsource will have to work, and, while doing so, will have no time left over for creating and innovating. Outsourcing is the great secret to solving problems. It gained momentum with the advent of consultancy services, which enabled the outsourcing of thought. Nowadays we pay others to think for us. It makes sense, considering no one is larger than their own shadow, and if I can use other people's skills and double or triple my shadow, why wouldn't I?

Many of the most profitable companies in the world ended up outsourcing everything, only holding on to the idea, the brand, and the royalties they yield. From toes to head, the higher up in your body you keep active in your profession, the more you'll earn. (This obviously does not apply to soccer players.)

So if you want to be successful in the madness that work has become, and have more time for creative and really productive idleness, I suggest you learn to outsource your problems and needs. In our society, and on a global scale, outsourcing has become an institution that goes from top to bottom of the productive pyramid, spreading out horizontally in all directions. However, like in easy money pyramid schemes, not everyone ends up fresh and happy. Somebody has to work in the ditches.

I came back from work that evening wondering if the ditch-digger and his hired hand had done the job. I found them both outside the ditch, each one leaning on their shovel and puffing their cigarettes. From the edge of the now-deep hole, a shovel would come up every once in a while, removing the soil. Someone was in there working. Through scarce nicotine-stained yellow teeth, they both puffed out in chorus:

"We outsourced!"

Behavior

'm fascinated by human behavior. Observing people, analyzing the fingerprints of every personality, trying to predict how they will act, these are all raw materials for those who write about marketing. Are people motivated solely by their needs? It's not that simple. Marketing studies the essence of human behavior — of people who are fueled by tangible as well as intangible forces.

Basic needs such as survival and preservation of the species have helped define the path of human behavior throughout history. Maslow studied this and even created a kind of hierarchy that went beyond physiological and security needs, drawing attention to those that involve such complex things as the heart, which has its reasons which reason knows nothing of.

Have you seen those cars that are powered by more than one kind of fuel? That's what we're like. In our brain tank, there's space for several motivational fuels, but there's also space for a powerful additive: the myth.

That's what I was trying to explain at a marketing class when a student told me what she had seen on Saturday at a party. Behind her was a couple who had just met and were having a lively conversation. He was bragging about his accomplishments, wanting to show that he was capable of providing for all the needs and expectations of the young girl. She laughed and splashed her charm around as she tried to unveil the exact pedigree of that potential Prince Charming. That was all part of a game as old as the human race — the courting game.

This game, which guarantees soap opera ratings and readership of novels, is also a game of attraction and repulsion. It's far too complex to explain, learn or teach, but its software is built in every human being that comes out of the assembly line. Fostering needs, desires and expectations as well as showing capacity to satisfy them is part of the essence and instinct of every living creature. In this seduction game, males and females dance to each other, like birds do; they exhale phero-mones charged with coded messages, as lions do, and they peck each other, like pigeons, before mating. All the while, they take notice of external signs of power or weakness in body features, colors and style of feather-ing.

Notice how fashion is designed to stimulate this game. In the traditional western way of dressing, men have flaunted ties for decades. Could they be a phallic symbol pointing to the genitals? Some people think so. Anyway, it helps to hide the shirt buttons and to keep the collar closed, pointing out that the neck, the most vulnerable part of the human being, is duly protected. A jacket with filling in the arms and long sleeves helps to convey the impression of muscles and virility. His looks should guarantee his capacity to provide protection for the female and their offspring, as well as strength and health for the preservation of the species.

In the meantime, the woman, more fragile by nature and bearer of eggs that must be fertilized in order to reproduce, displays her bare arms using sleeveless clothes, widens her neckline and adds on a collar to highlight her uncovered neck. "I am fragile and I am vulnerable," is the message she conveys to the opposite sex. Her looks should ensure the attraction of someone who can protect her and perpetuate the species. Animals, birds and insects have their own garments and ways of doing the same thing.

All this explanation would be too limited to the animal and physiological aspects if I didn't mention something that is apparently exclusive of human beings: the myth. The myth is the inaccessible, something everyone wants to be or have. Its strength isn't based on a logical rise, fueled by hard work, but, rather, by a lack of explanation on how one got there. It fascinates us to think that success is due to a combination of magical factors. That's why music and movie stars appeal so much to us. Every Argentina has its Evita, and every England has its Diana. They started from nothing and became everything in the minds and hearts of their people.

Another feature some myths have is their fragility, which further underscores the mystery of the origin of their power. That's the case of Luke Skywalker, from *"Star Wars,"* who is admired despite being the son of Darth Vader, the villain. So is little poor frail Frodo, from *"The Lord of the Rings,"* who attains power and glory by strikes of magic and luck, here and there. Once more, it's all explained by magic and the unexplainable. It's the same with novels about the poor Cinderella who meets Prince Charming and goes on to live happily ever after in luxury and opulence in a magic kingdom, where no one worries about income tax.

It's the way the human mind functions. Success explained by logic isn't appealing. Comic book superheroes were born during the Great Depression in the United States. They weren't heroes because of their efforts, and they didn't develop their strength and physique by working out at gyms and dieting. It was all magic and ... *"Shazam!"* they were flying. Bruce Wayne didn't move a pin to turn into the millionaire who was the real identity behind Batman. He simply inherited it all.

The myth will be all the more admired for some extravagance not allowed for simple mortals. I'm not talking about just wearing underpants over the trousers as Superman does. I'm talking about spending on superfluous things, like the celebrities do. We're amused by seeing artists light their cigars with hundred dollar bills, but we'd be shocked if we saw an industrialist doing the same. In our minds, the industrialist is real, having built his wealth through hard work, as any normal person would, while the artist is a myth, a fantasy, a dream come true by a sleight of hand.

From the outside of a culture, we fail to find a rational explanation for some spendthrift dictator who continues to get support from his people. He does it thanks to the power of myths. If pharaohs hadn't spent pyramids of money, they wouldn't have been worshipped by the rabble.

When a myth falls, another one takes over. Between 1799 and 1815, the European political panorama was centered around the charismatic figure of Napoleon Bonaparte. Who was Napoleon? A soldier who became emperor of France, with the same opulence and absolute power of the aristocracy that the revolution had defeated. Don't try to explain this using logic.

When I was 18, I used to go to dances at a club in my city. The other boys and I stood at a spot in the ballroom where we could be seen by the girls. Each one of us was swinging car keys in our hands to show freedom, independence and power. Even knowing that not one of us could afford a car, displaying the key was a sign of power. We were young people who, in a sleight of hand, became owners of cars. It's as if we had the power to say *"Shazam!"*, and things would simply show up. We didn't need to get into the club ballroom with a car; all we had to do was take the key. The key represented the myth.

It was a key that drew the attention of the girl in the story my student told me. The night was coming to an end and it was time to leave. That's when the girl revealed her need and desire: to be driven home by car. The boy produced a key from his pocket and offered to do just that. When she saw the key to her needs swinging in the air, reflecting the diffused lights of the club, she immediately liked the idea. This is where the story would have ended if things were simple. But they're not.

"What kind of car do you drive?", she asked in a sweet voice feigning a lack of interest, when in fact she was very interested in the race of the stallion she would ride on.

"It's a Beetle"

The name of the car was still lingering in the air as the prince saw himself turning into a frog in the girl's eyes. Nothing in the world would convince her of giving the kiss which would undo the curse the word "beetle" had brought upon the young man. She grabbed the arm of a friend who was conveniently passing by, asked for a ride and said goodbye to the dumbfounded ex-Prince Charming in a very brief manner:

"I'm gone!"

The boy thought it best to leave too. He glanced at his Volkswagen key, smiled wryly, and left.

On the way out, the couples were waiting as the valet service brought the cars. The prince turned frog was there, and so was the girl, who looked back at him with a snub nose of contempt. Before getting into her friend's car, a tacky-blue Aries, she looked back contemptuously at the failed suitor. That's when her smile turned yellow.

Right behind the Aries, the frog was regaining his princely image as he boarded a shining convertible New Beetle — the latest model. It was yellow too, like the last smile she gave him from the old junky model that was taking her home.

Improvising

My dad always impressed me. He was a master storyteller and a master of the art of finding simple solutions to day-to-day problems. These were, in fact, twin skills, because in order to tell stories or create things, one needs knowledge, imagination, and an advanced power of synthesis. In addition to that, considerable improvising skills are also needed, since those who tell stories or solve problems need to do it with what they have on hand, without any planning or rehearsing.

His hobby was inventing things. It wasn't about taking man to the moon or curing cancer. It was about finding simple solutions, using simple and easy-to-find things, to meet sometimes complex demands. Like a folding wheelchair, made of some iron parts, bicycle wheels, wood and canvas for the seat. After retiring, he manufactured about twenty of them in his home garage, just to give wings to imagination and wheels to the disabled poor. He used simple tools and a design totally lacking in luxury and sophistication. His goal was to solve, in a few hours, a problem some people had been facing their whole lives.

Then there were the lawn mowers, three or four of them, all made of parts from junkyards. I remember one of them, a small one, very light, with only one small wheel, made from a scythe handle, an electric motor from a floor-polisher, and a fishing line replacing the blade. It was used to cut off grass at small edges in the garden, where the big grass mower, the one he built with a water pump electric motor, couldn't reach. If I'd still been a child when the series was aired, I would have believed that my dad's profession, a bank employee, was just a cover for his secret identity: McGyver.

That's right, the one capable of performing the most amazing feats, using the simplest solutions. Using a chocolate bar to stop an acid leak, creating a magnifying glass with a looped piece of hair and white wine, or even making a lie detector with a blood pressure cuff and an alarm clock. The man was a human Swiss army knife!

If my dad was somewhat like McGyver, it happened naturally, effortlessly. For him, creating was something as natural as breathing. His regular job didn't require great ideas, and maybe it was the boredom of banking that made him take up a new identity when he arrived home. As a bank clerk he used to work in a completely predictable environment, where improvisation could not be encouraged. However, not all jobs are like that.

Nowadays, depending on what you do, it's hard to survive professionally without a fair amount of creativity and an enormous talent for improvising. People who are good at improvising are always on the lookout for new uses for everyday objects that have been around us for centuries. Have you ever eaten a cereal bar? Imagine how many people have had milk and cereals every morning and never thought about turning the cereal that came in a box into a cereal bar that can be put into one's pocket or eaten on a plane trip.

The recycling industry had its eyes on all the episodes of McGyver and turned itself into big business, making lucrative products out of garbage. Sandals made of used tires are now sold in high fashion shops and can cost more than shoes made of new materials. Art galleries are full of improvisations, made of cans, bottles and scrap metal. The ability to improvise with what you have is what makes the difference for many professionals who are over 40, with experiences that would not secure them a place in the job market if they were not duly recycled by competent minds.

A great barrier for improvisation is the desire for perfection. A pair of sandals made from tires would never meet all the conventional quality control requirements of the footwear industry. Nevertheless, for what it proposes to do, the sandal is perfect.

The software industry turned paying for unfinished and flawed products into a habit. They sometimes even ask for our help in their tests, by incorporating automatic information sending systems to the software in case of breakdowns. We use software that is not ready yet, knowing that the final version is yet to come. If these conditions were applied when purchasing an airline ticket, the passenger would agree to bear sole responsibility for his life and luggage if the plane were to crash. The truth of the matter is that if software companies waited for a full and stable version, they would never survive in this market. The speed of changes is so overwhelming that we will never see a definite version of anything again.

Not even you are living a definite version at this moment. Each time you get a new customer, take on a new position or start a new project, you know that you will face the unknown, that you won't have everything you need in order to conclude it, and that you'll only be able to finish it if you improvise.

People who sing or play musical instruments are familiar with the power of improvisation and the fact that circumstances interfere in presentations. The performance is always a little different from the rehearsal, and depending on the style, the more improvised it is, the better. If you intend to remain active in your profession, it's a good idea to work like people who play jazz.

The capacity for improvising is directly associated with creativity which, I believe, is an individual quality by nature. In spite of all the incentive for teamwork, the best ideas originate from private intelligence. Teams are good at developing ideas, but not having them. Take a look at what John Steinbeck wrote about creativity in his 1952 novel *"East of Eden"*:

"Our species is the only creative species, and it has only one creative instrument, the individual mind and spirit of a man. Nothing was ever created by two men. There are no good collaborations, whether in music, in art, in poetry, in mathemat-

ics, in philosophy. Once the miracle of creation has taken place, the group can build and extend it, but the group never invents anything. The preciousness lies in the lonely mind of a man."

In the text *"The Dumbness of Crowds"*, in her blog *"Creating Passionate Users"*, Kathy Sierra mentions James Surowiecki, author of *"The Wisdom of Crowds"*, as having said that *"while ants become smarter as the number of collaborators increases, humans become dumber"*. The idea is that teams can only produce ordinary ideas, while individuals are capable of coming up with extraordinary ones.

This is more or less what Brazilian author Ariano Suassuna said in an interview for flight magazine *"Almanaque"*: *"I read a lot, but only literature. Magazines make me a little anguished. Most of them are very frivolous and don't interest me. I abominate the so-called 'average taste'. I prefer bad taste to average taste. And most magazines cater to this damned average taste"*.

McGyver was one who stood out from the average crowd with ideas that, despite being put in practice with the aid of average people, had been conceived by him. He had the gift of always finding new uses for old things — the paper clip turned into a detonator and the powder soap box turned into an explosive. McGyver had the skill of seeing the possibilities beyond the common and obvious utilities of an object.

But the prize for this kind of ingenuity doesn't go to McGyver or my dad. It goes to Ms. Helena, our long-time cook. She was already quite old when her husband died. At that time, the wake was held in the living room, and it would have been a success, had it not been for the fact that the deceased was wearing a wig and that the sticking plasters, at that time, were not impervious to post-mortem sweat.

You guessed it — the wig slid out of place. But that didn't happen only once. It happened so many times throughout the night that the routine of the wake was affected. Nobody was crying, chatting or telling jokes. All eyes were on the wig, trying to guess when the next slip would be. And it slipped.

Patiently, Ms Helena stood up, walked to the coffin and put the wig back into place, trying to stabilize it with flowers. It was no use. Not even my father, who sat next to the widow, nor anyone else in the room, were able to find a creative solution to the problem.

Tired of waiting for McGyver, Ms. Helena decided to find a solution for the slipping wig. She asked everyone to leave the room for a few minutes and was left alone with the deceased. When we returned, the wig was firmly and permanently in place, to everyone's relief. My father whispered the question that was in every-one's mind:

"How did you do it?"

"It was simple," she replied, with a naughty smile. "I used a pin. I felt a little sorry for him, but then, dead people don't feel pain."

Quality of life

After hearing so much about quality of life, health, and good physical and mental condition, I thought it was about time to do something to shape up. Consultants, personal coaches. and public speakers like myself have a habit of giving people tips on how they should live. However, they usually come up with lots of excuses not to do what they profess. But there comes a time when you must walk the talk.

My first step was going to a health club that had just opened in my neighborhood. It was a really lavish place, with a pool and enough equipment to turn any rodent into Super Mouse. If you aren't familiar with Super Mouse, you must be a lot younger than me. If you are, the chances are you have a belly like mine.

I was amazed at the size of my belly when I saw myself on tape with no shirt on. They say that TV makes you fat. It does. That's what I got from the habit of eating while watching TV. I got fat. Nowadays I use up twice as much suntan lotion as I used to, just to cover the excess skin. I'm not on my own, however. More than one billion people worldwide are overweight, apart from 300 million who are fat or obese. Children are obese, and even the poor ones are driving up the statistics. Buy one of those super sized bags of potato chips, sold for a few cents in supermarkets, along with a big bottle of some cheap soft drink, and your hunger's out the door. It simultaneously overstuffs and undernourishes you.

The prevention of and fight against obesity have become big businesses. You need only watch the upsurge of the industry of wholesome foods, fitness equipment, and running shoes for the first and only stroll. Not to mention health spas, roto-rooter type fat elimination services — liposuction's the name — and weight-loss surgeries. That's the medical side of this food chain service which grows more than pregnant-looking bellies. What about the fashion industry? It's rolling in money. You're getting fat? Just buy a whole new wardrobe, newer and larger.

And it was because of my belly that I went to the health club to do some swimming. Those who see me today might not believe it, but I've won some medals in the sport. The girl who welcomed me was very friendly and showed me the schedule of available swimming hours. All I had to do was sign up and pay the membership fee, which I thought was unfair, since I'd be doing all the effort. Being tight-fisted, I struggled to convince myself that my incapacity to see my feet were a chronic ailment. I think I suffer from concentrated morbid obesity. It's all in the belly. That made me concerned about being detained at some US airport by the FBI, suspected of concealing a bomb.

I was about to sign up at the health club, when I decided to ask if I could swim at any day and time, according to my unpredictable touring speaker schedule. I couldn't. If I chose a schedule, the magnetic card would only release the turnstile at that time. Computerized turnstile thing. I loved it. I was really happy about the computerized turnstile. It was the excuse I needed not to sign up.

But my belly wouldn't stop growing and that began to bother me. Do you know what it's like to sleep face down and fall over sideways? Pregnant women do, but that's not my case. I made up my mind and went shopping around on foot for a treadmill. In the last shop I went to, I realized that it was the first shop that offered the best price, so I rushed back, almost two hours later. I arrived there breathless and revitalized by the long walk. I went in, made up some excuse for the salesman and went back home filled with satisfaction. Who needs a treadmill after walking two hours at a brisk pace?

Time went by and the belly got bigger and bigger. After reaching the conclusion that the output approach, that is, spending the excess calories, wouldn't work, I decided to do something about the input. The old strategy of curbing production when there's no demand. With all this in mind, I decided to start by the mouth.

That's when I got a present from my daughter, the book, *"The Food Revolution – How your diet can help save your life and our world."* My diet? What diet? I still didn't have a diet, but I got the message. My daughter knows my story. She knows about my involvement in the 70's, with counterculture movements that had nothing against culture. I thought I could change the world by spreading an ecological and preservationist conscience, words that could only be found then among those initiated in the field.

She knows that I only ate wholesome foods at the time. I wanted to save the whales and could climb up twice as many staircases with half the oxygen I need today. My daughter, a nurse committed to quality of living, must think there's still hope for me and for the world. So she sent the book with two goals in mind: to "...*save your life and our world*".

I decided to start with the "life" part and leave the "world" part for some other time. After trying the one-week diet — when all I lost was seven days — I decided to try a new approach. Coincidence or not, I lost three kilos just by reading the preface. From now on, it's all going to be wholesome and natural, like in the old days. I'm stuffing myself up with salads, and I can already notice the difference. Not only am I getting thinner, but I'm also getting greener.

Am I going to save money doing this? Not on your life! Have you ever been to a health food store? Losing weight without eating is more expensive than gaining weight by eating. Everything that has "Light" written on it weighs twice as much in our pockets, not to mention that you'll have to eat twice as much to feel satisfied. I've increased the "nourishment" item fourfold in my budget. Didn't I say it's a good business? Somebody's making money.

Riding the wave of the mad-cow psychosis, I announced that, in my home, meat only comes in walking or in a can, in this case only tuna fish and light sardines. And, as far as I'm concerned, the ox can sleep in peace. I'll keep him at least about 100 feet from my refrigerator. That's the distance from my kitchen to the barbecue place right across the street.

MARIO PERSONA

Fame

The headline of the article in the local newspaper screamed: "Gurus Charge Outrageous Speaking Fees." A while before, I had given an interview to a reporter who had asked me about the public speaking market. I shared my views as a guru apprentice. All of a sudden, I saw myself in that article, side by side with real gurus, like Tom Peters and Jack Welch. Side by side only in the newspapers, because in real life, I don't come close to earning what those icons charge for speaking.

Under the subtitle *"Public Speaker Has Released Five Books,"* the article mentioned that *"from a team of 120 gurus registered in a public speaker agency, Mario Persona is one of the most sought-after speakers, and his schedule is permanently booked up."* I don't know if I'm one of the most sought-after speakers, but I sure am all booked up. But just hold on a second. I have to take out the garbage.

There, I'm back. Where was I? Oh, yes, full schedule. It says that I receive two inquiries on average per day. That's also true. My name shows up on Google in some thousands of pages and, the last time I searched for the word "palestrante", which means "public speaker" in Portuguese, among more than one million results, there was my site in.... Well, you check it out. That obviously generates lots of proposals, but most of them don't follow through. Not even in my dreams. If only I were a real guru.

One day I'll make it. I'm getting ready. In order to become a guru you have to lie about your age — increasing it — and have gray hair — if there's any left. Having lived over half a century, that's how my hair's becoming. I ask the barber to only cut off the black hairs, but he doesn't always manage. When I get to be a guru, I'll have my own hairdresser.

I already have the black T-Shirt. That's what gurus wear beneath their jackets. In places where every other mortal has to wear a tie, the guru doesn't. He can afford not to. I bought mine at a gas station on the road, on my way to an event at a beach resort. I only had dress shirts in my suitcase, so I bought the black T-shirt, more appropriate for the beach climate. I also decided to buy it because I needed change for the toll fee. I didn't use it. I thought it best to wear the tie, which also conceals the belly.

When I become a guru, I'll take care of the belly, the double chin and the skin. I'll do a complete *lift-botox-lipo*. That's it. *Elder-silver* hair, sculptural body and *yacht-tanned* skin. Tanned on a private yacht next to a heliport, on a marina in the Caribbean. In the meantime, I'll work out pedaling on the lake. A guru's voice must be serene and steadfast, the pauses must be dramatic, a Zen smile on both lips and eyes. When it's time for botox, it's best to warn the doctor to leave some wrinkles at the corner of the eyes, so as to ensure the eye smile. However, it must be a mysterious smile, of the *"I know something you don't yet"* kind.

A guru should eventually leave modesty aside and ask big stuff, such as *"How Would You Move Mount Fuji?"*, as William Poundstone does in the title of his book, or create a flabbergasting project, such as Tom Peter's *"WOW!"* By the way, his name ends just like that, on his website, with an exclamation mark: *TomPeters! WOW!* What matters is being original, even if you use the old publishing trick of having a title that starts with numbers, such as Stephen Covey's *"The 7 Habits of Highly Effective People"* or David Niven's *"The 100 Secrets of Happy People."*

Originality is something I lack, and that's why I still consider myself a beta-version guru. Even for writing this short story I needed to borrow some ideas from John R. Brandt's article *"If I Were a Guru,"* published in *Industry Week*. I was reading in the bathroom, when, among other things the inspiration came. A real guru would never do that or, if he did, he would never let the public know. Newton humbly confessed: *"If I have seen further, it is by sitting on the shoulders of giants."* I did so by sitting on the toilet seat.

Gurus also get media attention. The article in the newspaper started with the phrase: *"Select club includes big shots, such as ex-presidents, but..."* No, it's not talking about me. I only saw myself after the *"but"*: *"but there's also room for lesser known people"*. That's where I come in.

I was once interviewed by a major business magazine. The reporter wanted to know about a company that had managed to overcome a market crisis. I spoke for one hour on the phone on the first day, and another hour on the second, because the reporter had forgotten to put new batteries in his tape recorder, something he would have never let happen in an interview with a real guru. I was really looking forward to seeing the interview published. I couldn't wait to read it. As soon as the magazine came out, I ran to the newsstand — a guru would never do that — to buy it. It was a letdown. One square hour of my wisdom was summarized in one quote: *"'It's amazing that the company managed to survive' says managing consultant Mario Persona"*. That must have been all the tape recorder managed to register.

In a way, it's a good thing that I'm not a full guru yet because I don't know if my ego would be able to deal with that. Not long ago, I was in an airport, at the boarding gate, about to fly to another speaking engagement. I was mentally building up what I intended to say, when something caught my attention. Did it have anything to do with me?

From the other side of the boarding gate, three people looked in my direction and talked amongst themselves, pointing to me. Did I know them? Nope, the young man and two women were complete strangers to me. Nevertheless, they continued pointing in my direction and exchanging comments. Instinctively I looked down and checked if my fly was undone, as I'd just left the rest room. They kept on looking. I checked if my hair was standing on end, but no. I was still the focus of their staring eyes.

Then I heard my ego whispering in my brain:

"It's you, Mario. They want an autograph."

"Do you really think so, ego?" I asked, slightly interested. "Why would anyone want my autograph?" I went on with my mental chat, while I checked if my pen was in my jacket pocket, just in case my ego was right.

"Come on, Mario. You write books, give speeches all over the country, and even have a thousand friends on Orkut. I know that deep down, you expected to become famous one day. Well, guess what? The day has come!"

The truth is that, sooner or later, we all become famous, even if only within the limits of our desk or at the homeowners' meeting. In the past, a human being in his lifetime, would influence about ten thousand people. Today, with all the technology available, that figure is much higher. For better or for worse.

Even if you're not a guru, you have to learn to deal with that. If I know that I'm capable of influencing so many people, what kind of person should I be? And if any anonymous citizen today can be filmed, photographed and tracked, isn't fame just around the corner? It is. A minor slip up is enough to make the headlines. Good or bad.

Every now and then I get an e-mail from some student who, in some way, I influenced some years back. I notice that he was influenced more for what he saw in me than for what I taught him. The fact that some student remembers me is fame. Good fame or bad fame, it's fame nevertheless.

During lunch at an event where I gave a sales presentation, I sat with two directors of the company that hired me, face to face with a sales professional. When I said that I had majored in architecture, she said that she had too. When I mentioned the school, it turned out to be the same one. When? Our classes had been together for at least three years. A coincidence such as this one could have turned out a big embarrassment, depending on the kind of reputation I'd left behind. Would I today want to say how I was in the past, or tomorrow, will I have to conceal the way I am today? That's what fame is.

None of that bothered me at that moment in the airport, while I was being pinpointed by those three people who, according to my ego, were dying to get my autograph. Since the distance was relatively lengthy, I even considered pulling myself a little closer, but I thought it might not look good.

Then I realized that I wouldn't have to. Only a few steps away, another group looked toward me. Man, wife and teenage daughter were whispering so I would hear what I was already hearing.

"It's him, I'm sure. Go there and ask him", said the mother, from the corner of her mouth.

"I'm shy, mom, only if you come with me", she whispered with a slightly blushed face.

I soon noticed that they didn't want an autograph. It was a picture they were after. This time, I was faster than my ego and was fixing my tie when they came in my direction.

"Can we take a picture?" they asked in chorus.

"Sure! It'll be a pleasure", answered a voice coming from behind, and taking the words from my mouth.

Soon mother and daughter photographed each other, all smiles, with their arms around the country singer I hadn't seen behind me. I must have looked like a fool. I tried to get in touch with my ego, but he told his secretary to say he wasn't in. I wasn't famous enough.

MARIO PERSONA

Exposition

One day you find out you need to let the world know you exist, so you decide to do something about it before your name only shows up in the obituary section. If this still hasn't happened, you'd better start getting along with the press, so you can become a source of information for journalists, and eventually help them in some story or interview.

There are many ways to appear in newspapers, but one should avoid the crime pages. It all begins by getting your name into the address book of a member of the press. Sure, this doesn't happen overnight. You have to offer something interesting for the press, something that isn't propaganda. If you're an expert in some area, it'll be easier to build up this relationship, writing about it in your blog, or sending your texts as a contribution to other sites. Some journalist might find your text while doing research and get in touch.

If you're not good at anything, don't despair. You don't have to be the best to get attention; you can even be the worst. The other day I saw a newspaper article about the worst football team in the world, the *Ibis Sport Club* of Pernambuco, in Brazil. See, there's hope for you too.

Let's say you're a worm expert. Some newspaper, site or magazine might want to interview you for articles such as *"Worms in the recovery of soil"*, *"Ecologically correct baits"*, or, perhaps in some sensationalist tabloid (the kind that presents rumors as news), *"Recipes for making hamburgers"*.

I know that, with so many blogs around, the odds are you won't find a reporter wanting to get in touch with you, unless you have a really impressive CV. One way to make that happen is to write one or more books on your field of expertise. With the resources available nowadays, anyone can either write or hire a ghost-writer, to put your ideas in print. There are several on-demand publishing services that can turn your book into a reality, even if you only publish one issue for each member of your family.

I don't mean you have to write a best-seller and sell millions, because your aim isn't being successful as a writer, but as a worm specialist. As amazing as this may sound, in our culture you're only considered an expert in something if you have published some work.

If you're not satisfied just to publish a book but would like to see it make the best seller list, then make up a title that starts with a number. How? Well you must have seen loads of them. They are generally self-help or do-it-yourself books, but I guess this could be done in any knowledge field. For instance, some people are successful writing about canine communication, as in the book *"101 Questions Your Dog Would Ask Its Vet"*. If it works with dogs, it should do the job with worms.

For those who love lists, there are titles for all tastes. However, care must be taken when choosing, because if you read one that I came across in a bookstore, you might not have time left for anything else: *"1,000 Places to See Before You Die: A Traveler's Life List."* If you're my age, you'd better skip the index, preface and acknowledgements, or you'll die before you finish reading. If you travel to these places on foot, you won't even need to read *"30 Days to Get Back in Shape."* If you have any time left, try learning *"Chinese in 10 Minutes a Day,"* but you won't be able to do that at the office of the doctor who read *"The 5-Minute Clinical Consult."* You'd better do it at home, where you can also take on *"Nietzsche in 90 Minutes"* and you'll still be left with *"30 Minutes to Solve a Problem."*

These titles aim to create a simplistic image of things by enumerating, categorizing and pigeonholing complex subjects in easy and seductive formulae Who wouldn't like to learn Chinese in 10 minutes or come to grasps with Nietzsche in less than two hours? I don't know what your problem is, but how much would you be willing to pay to solve it in just 30 minutes? Of course, that's the time it would take for a normal person, but if you're *"The One Minute Manager"*...

A book isn't necessarily bad just because it has a title with numbers. The title is often chosen by the editor, in order to boost sales. Someone lent me *"The 22 Immutable Laws of Marketing"* and I loved it. It must be just as good as *"The 100 Simple Secrets of Happy People"* and *"The 7 Habits of Highly Effective People,"* which I didn't read. I read the other one because someone was willing to lend it to me; I didn't read the other two because I didn't feel like buying them.

The thing is I don't like the cake recipe stuff. Not everything in life is simple enough to be taught with an "A, B, C" or "1, 2, 3," as women's magazine covers profess, in articles such as *"Ten Steps To Maintain a Relationship."* I know... in real life there are so many steps that you can never have enough shoes.

That's why when someone asks me for tips on how to write a book, I don't know what to say. I like the advice a writer gave to his son, when he was stuck with a composition about birds, which he would have to hand in at school the following day. Faced with a pile of books on birds, and staring at the blank page, he heard his father's advice: "Bird by bird, son; bird by bird." Today, *"Bird by Bird: Some Instructions on Writing and Life,"* by Anne Lamott, the kid's sister, is a best-seller.

Having a book published will help put you on the spotlight, not only in newspapers, sites and magazines, but also on radio and TV. Several talk shows like to interview experts in many different fields. Interviews can be live, taped, or even written, for printed media. It is important to be straightforward in everything you say, especially if your interview is edited, in order to avoid interpretation errors. If it's a phone interview, and you work at home as I do, be sure to take off your pajamas and put on something decent in order to feel well-groomed. This will help to build self-confidence, something that affects even the tone of your voice. There's no need to put on a tie or apply perfume. Phone interviews can be tough, if you're someone who can't talk with his eyes open or without walking around the room. OK, walk or close your eyes, just don't do both at the same time.

It's all more complicated on TV, because it involves image and body language. Especially if it's live. If you faint in front of the cameras, there's no way this can be edited. In any case, you might avoid a disaster by first talking to the reporter who will interview you, to know exactly how he plans to conduct the interview. I didn't, and that caused a big problem for me.

In 1998 I was the director of an Internet firm, which was a new thing and a much sought-after subject for TV interviews. The scenario was our company's booth at a trade show, with several computers in the background and kids browsing the Web. When the TV crew arrived, I immediately thought about what to say, because I wanted to calm down the mothers who were canceling our services due to an increasing concern over pornography on the Web. In order to turn things around, I prepared myself to highlight the importance of school research and the access to museums and encyclopedias. The reporter's mind, however, was elsewhere.

He arrived with his crew in the nick of time, and I didn't even have time to tell him what I intended to say. He immediately went on to tell me that he would make up the story that we had been browsing on some site, which would be a starting point for the subject we were about to discuss. They would broadcast live for that evening's news program. Three, two, one ...

We were immediately teleported to hundreds of homes, and seen by thousands of concerned mothers I was hoping to impress favorably.

Standing by the reporter, I smiled to the camera, a candid smile, which soured as soon as I heard the story he had just invented:

"Good evening, ladies and gentlemen, Mario Persona and I were browsing just now on the net, taking a peep at the chicks on the Playboy site..."

Virtual office

write as I travel, and I do travel! I've even thought about keeping a map on the wall, pinpointing the places I've been to, but that made me worry about the cost of pins. The way around it was to do some virtual pinpointing on some Web map service, reminding me of the places I've visited in different times and spaces. Sometimes I feel like those two characters from the old TV series *"The Time Tunnel"*, who couldn't go back home or the series would end, leaving the sponsors in the past. However, unlike Dr. Tony Newman — the one with the turtleneck sweater — and Dr. Doug Phillips — the one with the old-fashioned suit — I usually change clothes between one trip and another.

I stay in so many different hotels that I've given up memorizing the room numbers. At the reception desk, I always ask who I am and where I am. This really happened the other day. I left the hotel room taking with me only the key card, not the envelope with the room number on it. Halfway into the endless maze of corridors, surrounded by rows of perfectly identical doors, I decided to go back. But where to?

I came across an intercom and called the reception desk, but the clerk wouldn't tell me where I was, citing hotel safety policy. Since he couldn't be sure I was the one talking to him and staying at the hotel, the real me would have to show up at the reception desk to have my existence verified. I had to go there and produce a document that, fortunately, I had in my pocket, in order to have my face checked with the one in the photo and get back the number of the room I was already staying in. Or should have been staying in.

At least they were cautious and I like that in hotels. It gives you a feeling of security, even if it's only a feeling. The thing is that leaping from hotel to hotel makes you develop a kind of instinct for danger. For instance, I never step into the shower stall without checking if the floor is tiled or covered with some organic material. In a hotel, that boasted having had Juscelino Kubitschek, who was president of Brazil half a century ago, as one of its guests, the shower stall floor turned into an amalgam of dirt as soon as I turned on the shower. They probably never cleaned it up since the presidential visit.

I refused to shower in that mud, despite knowing it could have been presidential mud. Even so, there was something else I had to clean up. Something that was also contaminated by the hotel's lack of hygiene. Would you like me to explain? OK, get your barf bag ready. Well, imagine what one of those hollow plastic toilet seats can accumulate inside it when it's cracked. Can you picture that? Now think of what the weight of a seated body on top of it can do, and you'll have a pretty good idea of how desperate I was for a bath.

Don't think that I'm a very demanding customer. My only demand is a room with an Internet connection so I can hook up my laptop. No WiFi? A cable connection will do. No cable? I'll settle for a phone socket. The trouble is that some hotels are just not made for guests who work. In one hotel where I stayed, they thought of everything except the traveling worker. My room had cable TV, mini-bar, background music, hairdryer, iron and ironing board, and safe. Not to mention soaps, combs and shampoos, items we bring to our children even if we don't have any children. They thought of everything except for an accessible phone socket.

The manager informed me that there was an extra one, in the bathroom. Imagine how I would have loved to work sitting on the toilet seat, with my notebook on my lap! My instinct tells me a toilet is no place to work. I realized there was a phone connection behind the bed-table, however, when I pushed the bed away, I ended up finding the cleaning maid's secret stash. That's where she must've kept the raw material for her wig factory.

Now all I had to do was plug my notebook into an electrical outlet, to keep the battery from being used up. You guessed it. The power outlet was on the opposite wall to the phone, so I had to choose what to turn off, the TV or the minibar. The wire could barely reach it. I inaugurated my new virtual office balancing my notebook on a pile of pillows between two stretched wires, like clothes hanging on a line. Aren't hotels prepared for those who travel working or work traveling? That one wasn't.

In order to get to hotels such as that one, I have to go through flights, highways and certain situations. The only reason I don't complain is that it provides material for my stories. What would become of this book if I hadn't traveled by bus on the emergency lane of a highway in the interior of the state of Pernambuco, in Brazil? The driver wouldn't get off the emergency lane because there were so many holes in the paved highway. He commented that the solution was to cover them. I replied that it would be better to open a few more holes to make the highway flat.

I also discovered that there are holes in airline routes. Having a ticket bought by a thrifty client, I boarded an old Boeing 727 from an unknown company, only to find out that the plane had a hole in the aisle floor — a kind of viewing port under the carpet — from where you can check the landing gear system.

This is the kind of thing I like to find out about on Discovery Channel, on documentaries about disasters with other planes, but this time I was taking part in it, live. Or almost not. It was during a landing attempt, when the flight attendant raised the aisle carpet and laid down on the floor to look through the viewing port and check if the landing gear had locked correctly into place. That's right, lying face down on the floor, watched by dumbfounded passengers, during almost an hour, she shouted to the pilot in the cockpit:

"It hasn't locked! Try again!"

If the infrastructure for traveling is disappointing, the talent of the people is impressive. Paul, the driver who picked me up at the airport for a three-hour car ride to my destination, had prepared a basket with water, soft drinks, candy, newspapers and magazines for me. All of it in the back seat, where he insisted I stay. The biggest surprise was yet to come.

We were talking, and I soon found out that he had majored in geography, had a master's degree in tourism, gave lessons at college and owned a travel agency with several employees. Even so, Paul made it a point to drive his vans, cars and buses regularly so as to keep in touch with the needs and desires of his customers, in order to streamline his services. Now that was a real VIP service, done by a VIP and a five stars company.

Did I say five stars? Well, there are pitfalls in constellations too. I'll tell you something so you won't think I always stay at some fleabag hotel. The scenario now is a five-star resort on an idyllic beach. I end my lecture, tired out after so many trips, sleepless nights and airline snacks. All I want is to spend the whole afternoon sleeping and recovering. I close the room curtains, turn on the air conditioning, turn off my cell phone and jump on the bed ready for some magical sleep. At this point, I will consider your yawns as a result of my suggestion technique and not due to the monotony of my text.

My dreams are abruptly interrupted by the door bell. I jump out of bed and rush to the door in order to look through the peephole. Outside, the bellboy holds a message in his hand. What could it be? Some urgent communication? Problems with someone in my family? The worst comes to my mind. I cover my underwear with the first pair of pants I can find, open the door with my hair up, just to hear the young lad, with a posture of efficiency, announcing:

"Message for you, Mr Smith."

Blogosphere

W hen I created my blog, the "Mario Persona CAFE," I didn't imagine that I would publish nudity scenes. I found now that I am doing this systematically. Today I see that those who publish blogs expose themselves, get naked and even strip off those who don't. In the fairy tale, the emperor was naked and didn't know it. Today people and enterprises get naked, regardless of whether they know it or not. In the beginning of 2006 an article in a business magazine boasted: *"Blogs – YOUR ENTERPRISE IS NAKED – Blogs can be a threat or a great opportunity for your business."* The magazine revealed a trend that had been building up for years, one most people haven't woken up to yet.

Some years ago I adopted the blog for my business students as a tool of academic exercise. Each one created his own to make comments about subjects discussed in class, and today they are grateful for the vision they have gained through that. I heard about two of them that were called for job interviews, after their blogs were found by potential employers. The employers' opinion? They saw in this a characteristic of daring and modernity. But, don't think it was easy to adopt this tool for my students. Before that, I had to convince the faculty of its usefulness, so that its firewall would stop blocking the students' access to blog sites.

The communication of the future is the communication of the past — people talking with people who look like common people. Nothing sophisticated, nothing more, nothing less. Common people usually trust common people, and blogs offer this.

"Oh!" the skeptic might say, "How can we trust what the blogs say?"

You'd better not trust everything you find in them. However, this doesn't change their power and impact. In 2001 I read an article about *"The diary of Kaycee Nicole,"* a blog with the same name, then still known simply as diary. This one was a false diary, of a sick and non-existent girl, who died in the last message posted by a creative and lying mother. She moved thousands of readers describing, in the first person, the pains, the conflicts and the struggle of the fictitious teenager against cancer.

From then on, thousands of blogs have invaded the virtual space. Some of them are good, but most are only rough copy for banal subjects and have the duration of a nanosecond. But even those are useful for something. I once met a mother who worked all the week many miles from home and only saw her teenage children once a month, or every day at their blogs. They don't know that she knows their profile addresses, and neither do they imagine that she monitors they wanderings, knowing where they went, with whom they were and what they did there, through post and photos they publish. In their blogs they tell friends what they would never tell their mother, nor ever suspect her to be their most avid reader.

Every day someone finds a new use for blogs, especially due to the new stimulus it brought to the art of writing. When my daughter, Lia Persona Hadley, author of a book published in the form of a diary, studied nursing she developed a project called *"The use of the written language in the process of health care."* She researched the different effects of the act of writing on health and on people's well being. In the preface of her book, she wrote:

"Scientific research has demonstrated more concrete data regarding the efficiency of the use of the written language in the therapeutic process. The use of writing in health care gives the patient the chance to better express what he feels and thinks, when exploring the psychosocial field. Nursing could use this instrument in its practice."

In her text, I found expressions that describe practices used many years ago, even by those who ignored their therapeutic value, such as *"Poetry Therapy," "Poetic Medicine,"* and *"Creative Righting,"* a pur. describing the aim to heal people in a creative way through writing. Writing, as recreation and even as a cure, has been a secular practice that has now gained momentum thanks to an instantly publishable tool: the blog. The Therapy-diary is no innovation. Anne Frank was already doing that in the diary she wrote for no one to read, and the whole world ended up reading. The teenager exposed her fears, dreams and desires.

On July 15 1944 she wrote: *"...I feel that everything will change for the better, that this cruelty will also end ... I need to become attached to my ideals ... perhaps some day I can put them in practice."* Anne was killed because she was Jewish, but, while she was alive, her diary was her solace. Had the Internet already existed, Anne Frank would have written a blog. The therapy would have been the same, but she would have, in her informal hands, the media power. The same words that healed her fears and apprehensions would be whispered online, in real time. It would travel at thought speed. If they couldn't stop the cruelty, at least they would help heal the wounds of many other Annes.

The blogs will continue stripping souls. Every day millions of people will pour out their hearts, without any decency and for anyone who wants to listen, things they wouldn't tell their shrink. I have done this myself, in my different blogs, created in different moments, for different states of mind and purposes of expression. I write like an athlete, who needs to exercise himself. I write because, for the writer, writing is a physiological necessity.

I've already created several blogs to channel this urge to write and share thoughts. The first one was *"The Tora-Bora Manuscripts,"* a fiction blog I created in 2001, in which I took on the pseudonym of an Arab journalist — Ali Kilabah — in the middle of the Afghanistan war. It was a way of entertaining my late nights awake and getting relief from the tension of a difficult period I was going through. In it I rewrote the description of the combats that I had read about in the news and included Ali Kilabah as if he had taken part in the action. I was shocked to hear that my unpretentious literary exercise had been discovered by an Italian newspaper, that failed to realize that it was fiction and published the fact as if an Arab journalist had really been going along with the American troops. Later I found one or two debate forums where some people were trying to guess who Ali Kilabah was and what he was really doing in Afghanistan. Some of them even hinted that Ali Kilabah was the pseudonym of a terrorist!

Today, when I am not talking about marketing in my blog *Mario Persona CAFE*, you can find me hanging pictures in the gallery of *"The Painter in My Window,"* where I publish thoughts and pictures of different scenes of the sky seen through the window of my apartment. In the blog *"I Want to Tell..."* I once more take on a different identity and I write as if I were my son, who is disabled and unable to communicate, about how I imagine his world to be.

In my blogs, I can dress and undress as I please, and I feel well, naked or dressed, blushed or not. I think it is better like this, that the king know and admit that he is naked, than if others would have to warn him of his nudity.

However, blogs are not only teenage diaries or literary therapy for lonely nights. The professional and corporate blogs are gaining more and more strength. Although it is easy for a professional to create his own blog, things aren't as simple when it comes to corporate blogs. The problem is cultural.

When we talk about something related to business, we immediately associate it to an impersonal and boring language, to clichés and overused words such as "promptness," "security," or "reliability." Everything in those texts smell of advertising and human beings only show up in the form of models hired for staged photographs. Some corporations venture to create blogs that steer clear from the usual gobbledygook found in company sites, leaflets and advertising. Does anyone read them?

It's hard to imagine someone trading a personal blog, full of warmth, dreams and even word processing mistakes, for something that looks like a cereal box. Blogs have personality, they think like people, look like people and talk like people, not like trademarks. This is something companies must understand, when they create a blog, they are creating a kind of ombudsman, who will represent and eventually even defend its client readers.

The editor, who might be a ghost writer, an agency, a team or employee from the company, must be someone who knows how to deal with tricky situations, capable of listening to and accepting criticism, turning it into constructive dialogues for all. That's because blogs are two-way streets, where readers can interfere with their opinions.

This isn't easy. The blog might end up turning into a suggestion and complaint box — and you can expect more complaints than suggestions — or, to make matters worse, become more like an angry graffiti wall. If the person in charge of it is lacking in diplomatic skills, the blog might turn into a boxing ring or a lightning rod for all kinds of opinions contrary to the interests of the company. This, however, shouldn't discourage a professional or a company from having a blog. You will never know what the results will be until you've created your own blog. "Blogging" is a science we learn through practice. You see it's already become a verb and a science!

No one would think that a company might create a blog for any purpose other than an institutional one, for marketing its products and services, in order to boost sales. It wouldn't make any sense to invest so much time and money for the sole purpose of entertaining its readers. Obviously the professional blog exists as a channel of communication with its public, but seldom without revealing promotional objectives. These objectives, however, can never be guided by conventional methods of advertising.

I will give an example. Imagine that you have a blog in your enterprise and want to show how your satisfied clients managed to reduce labor costs after adopting the software you sell. You hire any advertising agency to create your blog and its readers will end up reading something like this:

"Our system has provided our clients savings of up to 30% of labor costs, being the best in its category, easily installed and so on ..."

Is it possible that someone would come back the following day to read a blog written by a creator of such advertising hogwash? I don't think so. Have you ever read a blog of that kind? Many, only once and never again, because the advertising language can't attract and captivate the attention of readers used to the spontaneity of the Internet. Nowadays it isn't a question of how much space in the media you are able to buy, but how much of people's attention you can attract. It is a challenge, because they are being constantly bombarded by information.

Even so, let's say that your company decided to give someone in their team carte blanche to be a CBO — Chief Blogger Officer — and let the guy talk to readers the same way a normal human being would. Instead of writing *"Our system provides so and so...,"* he would say something more or less like this:

"My goodness! There must be people out there wanting to have me for breakfast. That's because I heard about an enterprise, our client, that cut off 30% of personnel after having installed the system that me and the other fellows here developed. The worst part is that there will be people saying that they lost their job because of me. Is that possible?!"

Ok, it doesn't need to be so graphic and cruel, but it needs to be human. The important is that, besides being human, the blog look like and speak like we do. The corporate blog needs to respect the client's opinion and be friendly, leaving conventional scripts aside and taking on a human posture in its communication, something that many enterprises don't do, be it in the virtual world or not.

This became pretty clear to me one day, when I was at the lobby of a hotel, and a client, with a sleepy face, complained about the mattress to the manager.

"The mattress is horrible; I have back problems and can't sleep. I am dying of backache!"

Instead of sympathizing with her problem, by offering a replacement or a change of bedroom, the manager didn't hesitate and poured out his sales script.

"In that case, why don't you take the opportunity to visit our massage services?"

Aging

The concept of marketing has existed for thousands of years. It was in the shadow of one of the first trees, ancestor of the one that produced the paper for Philip Kotler's books, current reference source on the matter, that the first marketing action in history took place. In an exuberant Eden, where nothing was lacking, the same principles which rule modern marketing were applied for the first time. Which ones?

Discovering, analyzing, and satisfying desires, stimulating them or even creating them, by pressing the motivational buttons that make people act. No, Maslow was not there and his motivational theory was yet to be invented. But the buttons were there, and they generated desires and expectations for three basic needs: nourishment, pleasure, and prestige. Once pressed, the response was quick, and what happened next can be found recorded in *"The Book of Origins,"* known as Genesis:

"And when the woman saw that the tree was good for food, and a delight to the eyes, and to be desired to make one wise, she took of its fruit, and gave it to her husband." Genesis 3:6

Like what happens nowadays with money, the offer promised to guarantee support — *"good for food,"* provide esthetic pleasure — *"a delight to the eyes,"* and provide intellectual needs of self-esteem and realization — *"to make one wise."* What happened later is history.

When we see marketing transform itself into the latest fad of students or professionals, it is obvious that the one doing the marketing has the Force, including its dark side. The hedonistic brain of your client still has the same buttons as our Eden ancestors. Two thousand years ago they were republished, by the pen of the apostle John, with other names, but with the same effect:

"... because everything in the world, the desire of the flesh, the desire of the eyes, and the pride of life, is not of the Father but of the world." I John 2:16

These desires, for physical sustenance *("the desire of the flesh")*, for sensory pleasure *("the desire of the eyes"* or *"the greed of the eyes")*, and for intellectual pleasure *("the pride of life")*, are still the controls that motivate mankind. Once they are pressed, nothing can stop the human appetite. Our brain is hedonistic by nature, and satisfying those desires is priority zero on our list.

Therefore, the picture of a dying man on the cigarette package, as we see in Brazil and in over a dozen countries, does not prevent many people from smoking, nor can AIDS be completely wiped out with the diffusion of condom ads. When necessity is extreme, reason easily loses out to desire.

There is a fourth button that marketing explores. This one tries to convince the human mind that the other three can be pressed and enjoyed forever. It is the button that pushes old age and death to the corner. According to what a doctor I know calls "pop medicine," Juan Ponce de León wouldn't have needed to penetrate poisoned jungles to look for the fountain of youth. It was enough to visit the corner newsstand.

Recurrent magazine covers would have us believe that medicine has the cure for all ills. Well, for many it has, including for sleeping illnesses, caused by the tsetse fly, which devastates thousands of Africans. But, in this case, the substance which cures is used preferably in the manufacture of cosmetics. One makes more money by removing hairs from the feminine face in major first-world cities than by preventing the death of natives in the villages of Africa.

It is clear that we are all surfing the wave of cosmetic longevity, forgetting that gray hair has always been a symbol of wisdom in all cultures. Today it is dyed many colors and the dyes sometimes penetrate the brain, making its owner really believe that he has gone back in time. Wisdom is no longer the wave of the moment, and we let ourselves be influenced by public opinion, which is obviously made up of the younger majority. We have lost respect of aging, and now we idolize the teenagers' catwalk. A thousand panaceas are advertised, each promising each man and woman the enduring looks of an embalmed Lenin.

But, being born, growing, aging, and dying are stages of the same life that must be lived with dignity, before our body turns into fertilizer to ensure that animals, plants, and bacteria also have their chance of survival. Mainly bacteria. As I write, thousands of them wait — all of them with their mouths filled with saliva — looking forward to my eternal rest. Today I've swallowed some of their relatives; tomorrow it'll be my turn. Living is a hardheaded struggle and, no matter how many cosmetics we apply, the worms have been the winners so far.

Oh, yes, old man, old woman, what we need most is to learn how to age, and not think that burgundy-stained grey hair, tattoos camouflaged by hand spots, or piercings in flabby skin folds will make us teens again. The most important thing is to get ready for what comes next, since there is a fifth button that, when all others jam, still works in humans: the search for meaning in life and beyond.

While we are here, finding balance in aging is the middle way. For a professional, especially one who operates in the knowledge field, aging helps to add value, as long as he knows how to keep the brain wrinkle free, follow a diet of good deeds, and practice his communication on a daily basis. This last one is important in order to create a positive market interface. In the human process of learning and communication you find elements like data, information, and knowledge, but at the top of the professional pyramid value are experience and wisdom, things that only age is capable of producing. Like the best wines, it is something that takes time to reach its finest flavor.

Obviously, marketing will continue pressing our little buttons, because they are part of the weave of civilization itself. The positive side of marketing will continue to look for ways to minimize aging, to improve health, and increase well-being. Its dark side, however, will use deceptive means to make people believe they can become immune to death. This tragic marketing will continue trying to sell the dream that, in some secret lab, there is some kind of mutation process that turns ordinary people into superhuman beings. Yes, because this is another ancient human desire: to be God. Today, man turns to science, in the hope of getting there some day.

Stan Lee knew that when he created the *Incredible Hulk, Iron Man, Thor* and *X-Men*. But, not being expert in science, when he wanted to explain how a hero had come to existence, he took the first words that came to his mind — cosmic rays, radioactivity, or something like that — and these were immediately accepted by the faithful readers of his comics. This was how he explained the aberrations of heroes and villains in *X-Men*: they were mutants.

Maybe Stan Lee didn't know much about science, but he really knew how to read human behavior. It is not insignificant that the hero he helped create — *Spiderman* — is strong and powerful, but is also the perfect stereotype of the teenager: insecure, oppressed, reclusive, yet possessing an inner world so great that only by traveling hanging from spider webs was it possible to go everywhere. What for? Well, to save mankind and, of course, the little helpless girl. Raise your hand if you've never dreamed of rescuing a little helpless girl. If you're a woman, wouldn't it be just thrilling to be wrapped in a strong and secure Spiderman hug?

Wikipedia informs us that, after being advised by his wife not to obey the directives of his publishers, and instead to write like his intuition commanded, *"Lee gave his new superheroes a flawed humanity ... they could have bad tempers, melancholy fits, make normal human mistakes. They worried about paying their bills and impressing girlfriends, and would sometimes even get physically ill. Lee's superheroes captured the imagination of teens and young adults, and sales soared"*.

Understanding behaviors is good for the health of any profession. In a lecture for doctors, I presented my thesis that the public's perception of medicine is mutable. At present, it is no longer the cure that people look for. In the past it was, but nowadays cure is commodity, at least in the minds of the new generation, who think that anything can easily be cured.

This generation, that saw Luke Skywalker, from *Stars Wars*, getting a bionic hand to replace the one that was cut off by Darth Vader, thinks it is enough to know which button to press in order to gain extra lives. It is a generation that learns medicine on *Discovery Channel*, where the latest miraculous scientific discoveries are revealed in one program, followed by another showing a scientific team discovering a real dragon, the kind that blows fire from its nostrils, preserved in a glacier.

If the same TV shows a human ear being developed in the back of a mouse, what prevents them from doing the same with hearts, brains and bowels? It is only a matter of finding a bigger mouse. The new generation believes even that cryogenesis, which freezes crew members on fictional space trips, would already be a reality. But it is not. If it were, many people would be looking, in the frozen packing section of the supermarket. for a mother-in-law size plastic bag and try to convince her to start the process right now.

This is the perception people today have of medicine, though they would, in a rational way, deny it. The problem does not happen at the level of reason, but in an entire culture in which we end up immersed, thanks to technological resources that make no distinction between reality and fantasy.

If, on one hand, the media makes death commonplace, desensitizing us to its horror and finality, on the other hand, they create the illusion that is not an insurmountable barrier for mankind. Doctors admit that it is becoming more and more difficult to explain to families that a patient has died, because this option is not good enough anymore for those who think that science and technology have answers for everything.

This perception change happened mostly in the latter half of the 20th century. Some years back, headlines boasted newly discovered antibiotics, a solution for the infections that killed millions of victims of illnesses that are considered commonplace today. Headlines of this century promote medicines that streamline pleasure for a generation that thinks that curing illnesses has become a commodity and that good medicines must be blue. The new generation is hedonistic by nature.

When I was a boy, my hero was Dr. Christian Barnard, who made the first heart transplant. But who are the medical stars today? Plastic surgeons of Beverly Hills, from that TV show about overhauling women, like mechanics do who transform old cars, falling to pieces, into fast machines. People are more and more searching for absolute health and aesthetic immortality.

Not that this behavior has changed, but it is the fact that technology has managed to make some old dreams come true, and plastic surgery is one of them. In the past, rich women hired the best plastic surgeons of the time — the great master painters — to portray them naked. It is clear that the painters never dared paint the women as they really were, but rather created a graphic fantasy of what they would like to be. With their talent the artists were capable of turning old pyramids into delicate and well-polished diamonds. Instead of a scalpel they used a brush, and the effect of modern silicone was created with paint. Noble women also used to order a dressed version of the same picture, to cover the naked version hanging in the wall, in case the bishop dropped by. In some cases, the artists represented them as Greek goddesses, only to justify their public nudity.

In my opinion, the conversations overheard in the studios of the past were not very different from what is heard nowadays in plastic surgery clinics:

How many milliliters of paint do you want on the breasts? If you want, I can give a stroke here, another there and ... Presto! Facelift! Oops! The paint has dripped a little here ... no problem. We'll just do a liposuction.

Resilience

S pongeYou? Yes, that is you with a quality that is vital nowadays for any professional: to be a sponge. Any enterprise would want a professional like that, a SpongeYou to make its business shine. Do you think it is ridiculous to be a sponge? Nonsense, there is even one who became famous on TV, Sponge-Bob SquarePants. Don't even ask me, because I only saw SpongeBob once, in a glance, while "channel surfing" with my remote control. All I know is that he lives in a pineapple and works in an underwater fast-food outlet, literally mouth-watering its clients.

Leaving aside the TV SpongeBob, one of the most important qualities of SpongeYou is his ability to absorb knowledge, especially in difficult moments. Since in any business there are always difficult moments, pressure, abuse, and smear tactics, SpongeYou does well in these circumstances. The circumstances that put the squeeze on you are the same ones that allow SpongeYou to grow in adversity. Sponges are flexible, or as the highbrows of Human Resources would say, resilient. That's another fashionable word for you to absorb into your mental dictionary, which must already include empathy, synergy, sustainable development, and others.

Have you heard of resilience? It is the twin capacity to flexibility. It is resilience that allows an object to get back to its original state after suffering a deformation. Being resilient, the ball bounces and gains velocity, the spring propels the clock, and the elastic band holds the money together in the pack. You must know how to do all this in order to have value in the current labor market.

There are enterprises that like to use the terms "flexible" and "resilient" to describe a professional capable of holding up the load of eighteen others who were dismissed due to cost-cutting. It is not fair for them to use the word like that. While flexibility is useful for quickly adapting to situations, resilience functions as the memory needed to get back to the original state.

Having that memory of the original state is important so the professional does not let go of his essential values. When I was sixteen years old, I left Brazil to live in the USA through a cultural interchange program. In the airport I asked my mother what she wanted me to bring her when I came back. "The same son who left," she answered.

How do you recognize a real SpongeYou? It's easy, he is the anti-hero. He is frail and flexible, he yields under pressure, molds himself, adapts himself to the different environments and activities. He doesn't make a fuss when he falls, he is easy to deal with, and he doesn't like dirt. Why I don't I talk about knowledge? Well, he knows things, but not everything. He is full of empty spaces, or he wouldn't be a sponge. If he knew everything, how could he absorb new things?

Now, it is better to be a SpongeYou with two different textures, one to confront the heavy dirt and another one, softer and gentler to touch. Pick a SpongeYou of the 2M brand: Motivated and Moderated. If he were only motivated, he could smear the company's image with his lack of responsibility. You've already seen the guy who keeps going back and forth, shuffling paper around, looking busy and pretending to work? Well... on the other hand, if he's only a moderate, he might be a frightened guy, an alarmist who always avoids risks.

Have I missed any qualities? Yes, intelligence is essential. I've talked about moral upbringing, now I'm taking about intellectual upbringing, learning ability and acumen. That's not the same as having an academic background, since today degrees can be cheaply acquired. Moreover, a great deal of what is learned about business in universities is obsolete, something that some entrepreneur invented outside it. The best enterprises were created and are maintained by the most intelligent people, not necessarily by the ones who have more courses and diplomas. There is no leadership without intelligence, and an enterprise won't have a personality if it doesn't have intelligent leaders.

Lack of intelligence leads to servility, as opposed to a conscious, selfless, and humble service, typical of the great leaders who lead by their example. Servility is a frightened submission, just like the rats that, in the Grimm brothers' fable, followed the flutist of Hamlin until they drowned. Such people are easily pushed around and exploited by their bosses.

Another quality that SpongeYou must have is feeling good when he is lying on the floor. That's right, laughing at himself and remaining unaltered when humiliated. After all, sponges are also useful when washing the floor and some carpets are made from sponge material to absorb the mud and dust from the people that come into the house. Before you give up reading, you must know that there is some logic in this and that it will do you good to learn to behave like that, if you want to live well in a time of so much boasting and pride, especially in the top positions of organizations.

I read a news article about a Jewish artist who decided to launch an anti-Semitic cartoon contest. It was his answer to an Iranian newspaper which promoted an identical contest in response to an offensive publication to the Islamic world. According to the artist, ridiculing his own people was the best way to protest against the protests of the Moslems — it would be a kind of artistic-political-religious-cultural self-punishment. But there is a strategy in that. When Jews decide to ridicule Jews, whoever tries to do the same will only be helping the cause, going from opponent to ally.

It is not a new idea. It is the same principle of the suicide bomber, who blows himself up along with dozens of innocent victims. Who would be capable of applying capital punishment for murder to someone who has already done that? Self-sacrifice, self-harm, self-ridiculing — each is an action whose objective is to cancel any reaction. This can also be applied to many situations in life. People who ridicule themselves are not ridiculed.

I remember a school classmate who was always making fun of himself He was a real clown. What happened? Any student who came in the class uncombed, old-fashioned or with a ridiculous little hair in the chin, taking care of it as if it were the first beard, was immediately ridiculed by everybody. Not that friend of mine. He was not ridiculed by others. To be ridiculous was already his normal condition, so there was no room for others to ridicule him.

In my lectures I use this technique. Do you know those first five minutes in the beginning of a lecture? They are critical. In them you have the opportunity of winning or losing your public. If they consider you unpleasant, you are lost. It will be very difficult to conquer the public confidence after that. If you please them, the people will be inclined to forgive you more easily for a weak performance or some slip. If you assume a haughty attitude, you will be more inclined to fall and the haughtier you are, the bigger your fall. Come in low, on the floor, like a carpet, and there is only one way for you to go: up.

Right from the start of the lecture I begin to depreciate myself, generally in the form of a comment or telling a story in which I put myself in a ridiculous situation, or crosswise I reveal my total incapacity of understanding or doing something simple. When I ridicule myself I end up putting myself on the floor, leaving the audience without space to lower myself. So, I continue calm, using the vacuum of reaction that I perceive in the astonished looks, certain that nobody will think that I am worse than what I myself already think. It is the old gospel maxim that teaches that the one who humiliates himself will be glorified, and the one who glorifies himself will be humiliated.

In the movie *"8Mile"*, the character who plays the role of the singer Eminem does that when he beats his opponent in a duel between rappers. Before his adversary has a chance of speaking about his poverty, the debauchery of his mother, or about his girlfriend who was unfaithful to him and other humiliations in his life — things which certainly were in the list of the rhymes that the adversary would do — Eminem opened his life and revealed all that. After that, he threw the microphone at his opponent, with a challenge that literally silenced him:

"Now tell them something they don't know about me yet!"

If you observe an actor's performance, you will see that the humor technique is simple enough in nature. We laugh because someone got in trouble in a certain situation or because we were surprised by an unexpected conclusion. We laugh, in fact, when we feel good about the misfortunes of someone else and when we feel superior to someone's ignorance. We laugh when someone bangs their head on the signpost or is hit by a pie in the face. We laugh at blonde jokes, because that makes us feel more intelligent than them. And, when the joke finishes in an unexpected way, we laugh at ourselves for not having predicted the end. And that's what I'm talking about, being capable of laughing at yourself.

Whoever ridicules himself doesn't suffer. When he realizes that something is coming his way, he says right away:

"Boss, I am a jerk! An ass! I don't deserve to live! How could I do something foolish like that? You can beat, boss, beat me hard; I deserve it."

Who will hit someone like that? Nobody. If the boss happens to have a soft heart he might say something like this:

"Never mind, things like that happen, you even have talent, it is only a question of paying more attention..."

Laughing at yourself is healthy. It doesn't hurt. Do it. The next time you bang your forehead on a signpost, burst out laughing. If you look around, you will see that you are not alone. The people will love it and might even lend you a handkerchief for you to clean off the blood on your forehead or even ask you to play it again.

He who doesn't ridicule himself suffers. People who fear being ridiculous are generally insecure or have something to prove to themselves. It is probable that they are the ones who are always picking on others, being on the defensive or looking for someone to point their fingers at.

You must know someone like that. Someone who never admits something is his fault, never curves himself before the critics, is overbearing and uses heavy force, screams or takes advantage of his position to intimidate and to prevail.

I once saw someone like that. He had parked his shining VW Beetle in a no-parking space, right under the sign in a downtown square. His car was facing the square and had its back a couple meters from a big concrete light pole. As I walked by the square, he was debating with the policeman, who was about to give him a ticket.

"Do you know who you're talking to? This is not acceptable! I'm a friend of so-and-so!"

The policeman couldn't care less. He played dumb and kept on writing. Meanwhile, the discussion was beginning to attract a small audience for the little show that the driver was about to present. After receiving the fine, he jumped into the Beetle, mad with his humiliation, started the engine, reversed gears and sped away backwards. The squealing of the tires caught the attention of more people, increasing the audience of a scene worthy of *"The Three Stooges"*, but which he was bent on playing all by himself.

In order not to infringe on the laws of physics, which hold that two bodies cannot simultaneously be at the same place at the same time, the back of the Beetle embraced the concrete light pole as if they were old friends, and the engine decided to move to the backseat. The driver was furious as he got out of the car and, not being able to unload his wrath on the law officer, who was laughing uncontrollably, he started kicking the light pole and cursing its mother.

Acknowledgments

This section usually comes at the beginning of the book, not at the end. I left it for the end, however, because I considered it the best part of what I had to say. The person I am most grateful to is my personal coach, and that's what I want to talk about here.

This is the definition I got from the Internet: *"a personal coach is a personal consultant, a facilitator who helps his/her client develop what's best in him/her, and, consequently, to achieve his/her professional and personal goals."* I searched for this definition because I wanted to be sure, and now I am, that I've had a personal coach. Do you? If you intend to hire one, choose someone you're a fan of.

If Philip Kotler were available, I would have hired him as a personal coach, to teach me how to write about marketing, or Peter Drucker, to teach me business management. I would have looked for Tom Peters, to get some tips on people management, and I would set some time aside to learn with Dave Barry to do all this in the form of good spirited short stories. Unfortunately, it wasn't possible.

I admire all those people, but none of them were my personal coaches, neither did any of them stimulate me to write and become what I am today. Even so, I still had a personal coach, who always encouraged me to become a writer. Don't tell any of them, we don't want to hurt their feelings, but I consider her to be — that's right, it's a woman — better than all of them put together. Much better.

The professional who prepared me to be what I am today never wrote books, never made speeches and never taught in colleges. She simply got involved, committed and dedicated herself to the mission of making me somebody, and she always encouraged me to write, believing one day I'd be a writer. She always read my texts, making suggestions, criticizing a thing or two, but, above all, she thought I should always go on, never give up.

I remember a composition I wrote in junior school, which she kept for many years and frequently referred to. That was the first text I wrote without fear of getting a low grade. I reckoned creating a piece of writing full of sarcasm and good spirits was a risk worth taking. I described every detail of the classroom, pointing out the dust and the spider webs on the ceiling. As far as I can remember, it was my first text using metaphors and analogies. I don't remember how, but I compared my class to a battlefield in Vietnam. The teacher liked it.

Oddly enough, unlike what happens in a coaching job, my personal coach didn't charge a cent for full-time training. She had to give up a lot of things in order to help in my personal and professional development. That included a commercial career, where she could have made very good use of her incredible business skills. She never regretted that. On the contrary, she always taught me to value long-term investments.

I remember a time, almost forty years ago, when my personal coach set out on a more ambitious path, going beyond the services she rendered in the home office. She opened up a boutique and started making money. Coming from a home where her parents were successful in the footwear industry, deals and entrepreneurship were in her DNA. She did the right thing professionally.

On a personal basis, however, that turned out to be a mistake. She realized that her business was getting in the way of her relationship with her partner and compromising the quality of her coaching services to her three main clients: me and my two sisters. That was when our personal coach decided to give up her own career, forfeiting financial gain in the present in order to invest her time exclusively in other careers of future value.

Today I even sense a feeling of relief for not having hired Philip Kotler, Peter Drucker or Tom Peters. They're good, but her performance as my personal coach was much better. On February 16, 2005 she, who always encouraged me to write, terminated a longtime contract with me and my sisters. On the same day that my fifth book was leaving the publishing house on the way to the bookstores, she was leaving for her final resting place, heaven.

Her name, Ruth Buzolin Persona, was never preceded by professor, doctor, consultant, or any other title earned with degrees, theses or monographs. I always called my personal coach simply mom.

Did you like the book? Contact the author:

Mario Persona

contato@mariopersona.com.br

www.mariopersona.com.br